Edinburgn, Pentlands and Lothians

Walks

*Compiled by
Terry Marsh*

Acknowledgements
The publisher would like to thank Beverley Stirling at Beecraigs Country Park and
the Rangers at Almondell and Calderwood Country Park for their advice.

Text: Terry Marsh
Photography: Terry Marsh, Brian Conduit, John Brooks, Dennis Kelsall
Editorial: Ark Creative (UK) Ltd
Design: Ark Creative (UK) Ltd

This product includes mapping data licensed from Ordnance
Survey® with the permission of the Controller of Her
Majesty's Stationery Office. © Crown Copyright 2010. All
rights reserved. Licence number 150002047. Ordnance Survey, the OS symbol
and Pathfinder are registered trademarks and Explorer, Landranger and Outdoor
Leisure are trademarks of the Ordnance Survey, the national mapping agency of
Great Britain.

ISBN: 978-1-85458-534-9

While every care has been taken to ensure the accuracy of the route directions,
the publishers cannot accept responsibility for errors or omissions, or for changes
in details given. The countryside is not static: hedges and fences can be removed,
field boundaries can alter, footpaths can be rerouted and changes in ownership
can result in the closure or diversion of some concessionary paths. Also, paths
that are easy and pleasant for walking in fine conditions may become slippery,
muddy and difficult in wet weather, while stepping stones across rivers and
streams may become impassable.

    If you find an inaccuracy in either the text or maps, please write to Crimson
Publishing at the address below.

First published 2001 by Jarrold Publishing
Revised and reprinted 2006, 2010

Printed in Singapore. 3/10

First published in Great Britain 2010 by Crimson Publishing,
a division of:
Crimson Business Ltd,
Westminster House, Kew Road, Richmond, Surrey, TW9 2ND

www.totalwalking.co.uk

A catalogue record for this book is available from the British library.

Front cover: Priestlaw Hill
Previous page: Edinburgh Castle

Contents

Walkers and the Law;
Glossary of Gaelic Names;
Safety on the Hills;
Useful Organisations;
Ordnance Survey Maps

Approximate walk times

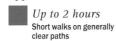 **Up to 2 hours**
Short walks on generally clear paths

 **2½–3½ hours**
Slightly harder walks of moderate length

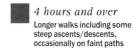 **4 hours and over**
Longer walks including some steep ascents/descents, occasionally on faint paths

The walk times are provided as a guide only and are calculated using an average walking speed of 2½mph (4km/h), adding one minute for each 10m (33ft) of ascent, and then rounding the result to the nearest half hour.

Walks are considered to be dog friendly unless specified.

Keymap 1

SCALE 1:250 000 or 1 INCH to 4 MILES *1CM to 2.5KM*

0 2 4 6 8 10 KILOMETRES 15

0 2 4 6 MILES 8 10

KEYMAP HEIGHTS SHOWN IN METRES

KINROSS
Kinross Services
Loch Leven
St Serf's Island
Lochleven Castle
Priory
Gairney Bank
Ballingry
Benarty Hill
Lochore
Glencraig
Kelty
LOCHGELLY
Lumphinnans
COWD
Hill of Beath
Crossgates
Donibristle
Fordell
Townhill
Milesmark
DUNFERMLINE
Wellwood
Gowkhall
Carnock
Oakley
Cowstrandburn
Crossford
Fordell Castle
Hilend
St Bridget's Kirk
DALGETY BAY
INVERKEITHING
Inverkeithing Bay
North Queensferry
Inch Garvie
Barnbougle Castle
Dalmeny House
Forth Road Bridge
Forth Bridge
Dalmeny
QUEENSFERRY Services
Newton
Dundas Castle
Kirkliston
Edinburgh Airport
Cramond Bridge
Turnhouse
Gogar
Ingliston
A90
Ratho Station
Newbridge
Ratho
Bonnington
Suntrap
Hermiston
Juniper Green
CURRIE
Malleny House
Balerno
LIVINGSTON
Mid Calder
East Calder
Wilkieston
Kirknewton
Oakbank
Dedridge
Murieston
Bellsquarry
Threipmuir Reservoir
Black Hill
Scald Law
BATHGATE
Boghall
Deans
Livingston Village
Seafield
ARMADALE
Whiteside
Blackburn
East Whitburn
WHITBURN
Stoneyburn
Addiewell
Polbeth
West Calder
Harperrig Reservoir
Bore Stane
Nine Mile
Morton Reservoir
Harthill Services
Eastfield
Harthill
Longridge
Loganlea
Greenburn
Breich
Fauldhouse
Stane
Forth
Stobwood
Auchengray
Tarbrax
Wilsontown
Climpy
Rootpark
Woolfords Cottages
Cobbinshaw Reservoir
Crosswood Reservoir
ROMAN FORTLET
Baddinsgill Reservoir
Carlops
West Water Reservoir
Mendick Hill
West Linton
Romanno Bridge
PENTLAND HILLS
White Craig
Bleak Law
Byrehope Mount
Hendry's Corse
Braehead
Netherton
West Mains
Dunsyre
Yieldshields
Roadmeetings
Harelaw
Springfield Reservoir
Hare Hill

DOLLAR
Burnfoot
Lendrick Hill
Carnbo
A91
Commonedge
River Devon
Devonside
Coalsnaughton
Sauchie
Keilarsbrae
CLACKMANNAN
Kennet
Clackmannanshire Bridge
A977
A876
Airth
Kincardine
Devilla Forest
Moor Loch
Kincardine on Forth Bridge
Blair Castle
Power Sta
Longannet Point
CULROSS
Abbey
Valleyfield
Low Torry
Torryburn
Torry Bay
Crombie
Charlestown
Limekilns
ROSYTH
Europarc
St Margaret's Hope
Hopetoun House
Blackness
Castle
Carriden
Muirhouses
BO'NESS
GRANGEMOUTH
Skinflats
A905
Redding
Polmont
Brightons
Maddiston
Loan
Blackbraes
Standburn
Westfield
Linlithgow Bridge
Whitecross
LINLITHGOW
Linlithgow Palace
Philpstoun
Old Philpstoun
Kingscavil
Bridgend
Winchburgh
Ecclesmachan
Broxburn
Uphall
Burnside
Newton
Champany
The Binns
Dechmont
Wester Dechmont
Torphichen
Loan
Blairingone
Cult Hill
Hill End
Cleish
Cleish Hills
Fort
Knock Hill
Saline
Balgonar
Craigluscar Hill
Bowershall
Kingseat
Bothkennar
Kinneil House

MORRAN ROAD

FIRK
Redding
M9
M90
B914
Loch Fitty

Pitkevy
Balfarg
Star
Lundin Links
Kirton of Largo or Upper Largo
Holl Resr
Arnot Resr
LESLIE
Cadham
MARKINCH
Milton of Balgonie
Kennoway
Bonnybank
A915
Lower Largo
Drumeldrie
Colinsburgh
13 A917
GLENROTHES
15
Castle
Balcurvie
LEVEN
Largo Bay
Ruddons Point
Earlsferry
Chap Nes
Kinglassie
B922
Windygates
A911
METHIL
B9130
Thornton
Coaltown of Balgonie
A915
BUCKHAVEN
Dogton
Stone Cross
B921
Macduff's Castle
River Ore
B9130
A92
Coaltown of Wemyss
East Wemyss
Auchterderran
Cluny
A955
West Wemyss
Gallatown
B981
A92
B981
Dysart
Chapel
A910
Ravenscraig Castle
Loch Gelly
B925
Pathhead
KIRKCALDY
DENBEATH
Auchtertool
Linktown
B9157
Seafield Tower
Stenhouse Reservoir
B923
KINGHORN
A909
A921
Pettycur
Castle
Aberdour
BURNTISLAND

FIRTH OF FORTH

Inchkeith
Inchcolm
Oxcars
Inchmickery
Eyebroug
Gullane Bay
25
Aberlady Bay
Aberlady
Cramond Island
Gosford Bay
Gosford House
Spittal
Cramond
Granton
Black Rocks
Ocean Terminal
Leith
COCKENZIE AND PORT SETON
A198
Longniddry
B9085
EDINBURGH
12
PRESTONPANS
22
B6363
Elvingston
Corstorphine
Castle
6
PRESTONPANS
Power Sta
1745
Gladsmuir
Morningside
Portobello
MUSSELBURGH
A199
A1
12
Penston
Macmerry
Craiglockhart
16
Inveresk
Wallyford
A199
New Winton
New Town
Colinton
Fairmilehead
Braid Hills
A772
Liberton
Craigmillar Castle
Edinburgh Services
A7
Danderhall
Millerhill
Whitecraig
Elphinstone
B6371
1567
144
Ormiston
B6355
Winton House
Redmains
TRANENT
14
East Saltou
Dregh
Servic
ermuir
Hill
17
A720
Kaimes
Gilmerton
A6094
Crossgatehall
B6414
Cousland
96
14
Pencaitland
18
5
Stralton
A768
LOANHEAD
Eskbank
DALKEITH
A6106
A68
Peastonbank
Peaston
West Saltou
Gilchriston
Woodhouselee
Ca
15
Easter Howgate
Milton Bridge
Roslin
Bilston
Castle
A6094
LASSWADE
BONNYRIGG
Edgehead
Cranstoun Riddel
Pathhead
Leaston
Humbie
Stobshiel
Blegbie
A703
Mayfield
8
Dalhousie Castle
Newtongrange
Dewartown
B6372
B6458
Fala Dam
Fala
23
A702
Auchendinny
Rosewelt
Arniston
Newlandrig
Crichton
Castle
B6367
Loganlea Reservoir
Castle
Arniston House
Gorebridge
B479
A766
River North Esk
PENICUIK
Carrington
Borthwick
Tynehead
451
Mile Burn
A701
Howgate
Edgelaw Reservoir
North Middleton
Temple
Fala Moor
A68
Auchencorth Moss
Leadburn
B6372
Rosebery Reservoir
Middleton
Gilston
415
ROMAN ROAD
B6368
A703
B7007
Torfichen Hill
460
Heriot
27
A7
468
Lamancha
27
Gladhouse Reservoir
Forts
382
Collie Law
Waterheads
MOORFOOT HILLS
651
Blackhope
Dewar
Dun Law
515
Fountainhall
Torquhan
305
356
A68

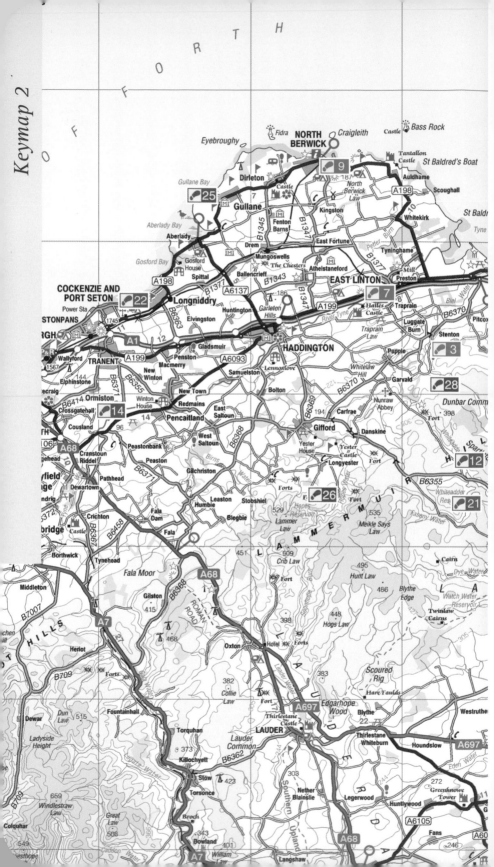

SCALE 1:250 000 or 1 INCH to 4 MILES *1CM to 2.5KM*

0 2 4 6 8 10 KILOMETRES 15

0 2 4 6 MILES 8 10

KEYMAP HEIGHTS SHOWN IN METRES

ed's Cradle
Mouth

2
DUNBAR
Broxburn
West Barns
Barns Ness
1296 1650
Spott
Brunt Hill 225
Halls
Dry Burn
Cement Works
Skateraw
Torness Point
Power Sta
Thorntonloch
Innerwick Castle
A1
Reed Point
Pease Bay
Siccar Point
Dunglass Church
Cockburnspath
Oldhamstocks
319
Cocklaw Hill
Ecclaw
Fort
245
Meikle Black Law
Wheat Stack
East Castle
Telegraph Hill
Lumsdaine
ST ABB'S HEAD
227 Cross Law
Forts
Northfield
St Abbs
397
Bransly Hill
19
art aw
391
277
Upland Way
Blackburn Rig
Grantshouse
A1107
Coldingham Moor
12
St Abbs
Priory
Coldingham Bay
LS
Bothwell Water
Edge
Coldingham
B6438
Ale
Water
379
Cranshaws Hill
Cranshaws
Ellemford
Abbey St Bathans
Broch
Fort
Fort
Fort
262
Horseley Hill
Houndwood
Water
19
Cairncross
B6438
Marygold
Auchencrow
Reston
Ayton
A1
B6355
Longformacus
B6365
Lintlaw
Preston
B6355
217
Dirrington Great Law
Duns Castle
Chirnsidebridge
Church Edrom
Chirnside
Lamberton
Foulden
Clappers Halidon Hill
A6105
Whiteadder Water
1333
Dirrington Little Law
244
DUNS
Gavinton
Manderston House
Blackadder
Allanton
Hutton
50 B6460
Paxton
B6461
Choicelee
Polwarth
Whitsome
New Horndean
Paxton House
Fishwick
River Tweed
Loanend
Longridge Towers
Halliburton
Hule Moss 285
A6105
Fogo
B6460
Blackadder Water
Horndean
Ladykirk
Castle
Thornton Park
Horncliffe
Murton
Thornton
Shoresdean
Greenlaw
Fogorig
Swinton
Norham
Shoreswood
A697
Purves Hall
Swintonmill
Upsettlington
Simprim
B6470
Grindon
B6354
Felkington
Leitholm
A6112
B6437
A698
109
Hume
Hume Castle 223
Sweethope
Lambden
Orange Lane
Eccles
269
Lennel
Cornhill on Tweed
Castle Heaton
Pallinsburn House
Duddo
Etal Castle
Etal
Legars
Birgham
COLDSTREAM
Hay

Walk	Page	Start	Nat. Grid Reference	Distance	Time	Height Gain
Aberlady Nature Reserve and Gullane Bay	78	Aberlady	NT 471805	8 miles (13km)	4 hrs	555ft (170m)
Allermuir Hill and Capelaw Hill	54	Swanston	NT 240674	5 miles (8km)	3 hrs	1,295ft (395m)
Arthur's Seat	25	Palace of Holyroodhouse	NT 271737	3½ miles (5.5km)	2 hrs	1,080ft (330m)
Beecraigs and Cockleroy	34	Beecraigs Country Park	NT 007746	4½ miles (7.2km)	2½ hrs	575ft (175m)
Bonaly Country Park and Harbour Hill	57	Bonaly Country Park	NT 212676	5½ miles (9km)	3 hrs	1,015ft (310m)
Braid Hills	51	Blackford	NT 255709	5 miles (8km)	2½ hrs	1,000ft (305m)
Caerketton Hill	22	Boghall Farm	NT 245652	3 miles (5km)	2 hrs	1,000ft (305m)
Carlops and North Esk Reservoir	37	Carlops	NT 161559	4½ miles (7km)	2½ hrs	835ft (255m)
Dunbar and Belhaven Bay	16	Dunbar	NT 679791	2½ miles (4.7km)	1½ hrs	275ft (85m)
Dunbar Common and the Herring Road	89	Pressmennan Wood	NT 621726	11¼ miles (18km)	6 hrs	1,625ft (495m)
Gamelshiel Castle and Whiteadder Water	40	Whiteadder Reservoir	NT 646642	4½ miles (7km)	2½ hrs	855ft (260m)
Gladhouse Reservoir and the Huntly Cot Hills	85	Gladhouse Reservoir	NT 309541	9 miles (14.5km)	4½ hrs	1,130ft (345m)
Glencorse Reservoir and Castlelaw Hill Fort	48	Flotterstone	NT 233631	5 miles (8km)	2½ hrs	835ft (255m)
Hailes Castle	28	East Linton	NT 591774	3¾ miles (6km)	2 hrs	310ft (95m)
John Muir Way	68	Cockenzie	NT 391750	7½ miles (12km)	3½ hrs	165ft (50m)
Lammer Law and the Hopes Reservoir	81	Longyester	NT 549655	8¾ miles (14km)	4½ hrs	1,460ft (445m)
Linlithgow Loch	14	Linlithgow	NT 002772	2½ miles (4.2km)	1 hr	165ft (50m)
Monks Rig and West Kip	42	Nine Mile Burn	NT 177577	4½ miles (7km)	2½ hrs	1,165ft (355m)
Monynut Edge	60	Upper Monynut Forest	NT 694676	5½ miles (8.8km)	3 hrs	1,065ft (325m)
North Berwick Law	32	North Berwick	NT 553842	3¾ miles (6km)	2 hrs	675ft (205m)
Pencaitland Railway Walk	44	Crossgatehall	NT 371689	5 miles (8.2km)	2½ hrs	130ft (40m)
Pentland Ridge and Logan Burn	71	Flotterstone	NT 233631	6¾ miles (11km)	4 hrs	1,755ft (535m)
Pressmennan Wood and Lake	18	Pressmennan Lake	NT 622726	3 miles (4.8km)	1½ hrs	605ft (185m)
Priestlaw Hill	65	Whiteadder Reservoir	NT 646642	6½ miles (10.5km)	3½ hrs	1,000ft (305m)
River Almond Walk	62	East Calder	NT 092682	5¾ miles (9.2km)	3 hrs	575ft (175m)
Roslin Glen Country Park	30	Roslin Glen	NT 273628	3¾ miles (6km)	2 hrs	490ft (150m)
Scald Hill and two Kips	74	Threipmuir Reservoir	NT 166639	7½ miles (12km)	4 hrs	1,885ft (575m)
Threipmuir and Harlaw Reservoirs	20	Threipmuir Reservoir	NT 166639	3½ miles (5.5km)	1½ hrs	130ft (40m)

A splendid romp along a delightful coastline that is hugely popular with birdlife, and a Site of Special Scientific Interest.

A steep and steady climb to a stunning vantage point, both north and south. An extension leads west to embrace a minor hill before the route slips northwards.

The walk up onto Arthur's Seat rewards with a commanding view of considerable extent; it is briefly steep in places, but this circuit combines sections that are energising with bouts of easier walking.

Not surprisingly, this is a popular place at weekends with city dwellers. The brief haul onto Cockleroy is well worth the effort, and is one of the finest viewpoints in lowland Scotland.

Starting from the very suburbs of Edinburgh, this easy and interesting walk leads south into the edges of the Pentland Hills, passing reservoirs and following a track across the hills before returning to Bonaly.

This short but energetic walk takes you to one of the finest viewpoints of 'Auld Reekie', as Edinburgh is known. But the view from the top of the Braid Hills reaches way beyond Loch Lomond.

A steady uphill climb to a comparatively modest hill rewards with a stunning view over the city of Edinburgh and across the Firth of Forth. Caerketton Hill is arguably the site of a Bronze Age burial cairn.

This walk is a delightful ramble into the folds of the Pentland Hills. Some climbing is involved, but it is not overly demanding, and is a splendid introduction to walking among these appetising hills.

A charming walk along the coast to the west of Dunbar, following a section of the John Muir Way before returning to Dunbar by a quiet back road. A good walk for birdwatching.

A taste of wild moorland; the ascents and descents on this walk are gentle, and allow plenty of time to take in the magnificent moorland views. *Not advised in poor visibility.*

These spartan hills are lonely, haunted by curlew and golden plover. Anyone seeking solitude will find it in abundance here.

The Moorfoots are the least well known of the hills to the south of Edinburgh, but they host excellent walking. There is a steady climb to the ridge, but the reward is one of fine views.

A most agreeable walk along the side of a reservoir, leading to a short climb to a superb terrace path above the valley. The walk concludes with a visit to an Iron Age hill fort and earth house.

An easy and delightful walk in the company of the River Tyne, to one of Scotland's oldest castles. The return leg follows a narrow country lane, high above the river.

An easy ramble along a stunning coastline, much favoured by birds throughout the year; binoculars are essential. A relaxing and enjoyable walk well served by public transport.

The combination of a challenging ascent to the highest summit of the Lammermuir Hills, enhanced by a walk in a secluded valley, following the course of a burn to a reservoir, makes this a rewarding outing.

The historic palace of Linlithgow and the adjacent Church of St Michael, one of the finest in Scotland, are always in view on this undemanding and delightful lochside walk.

A long and steady pull from the valley of the North Esk leads up to the end of the main Pentland ridge; this is a quite special place, and the whole range of the Pentlands a walker's delight.

A forest trail runs above a burn, providing views of a beautiful landscape. *The return over Heart Law demands good navigational skills, and this section should not be attempted in poor visibility.*

The climb comes right at the start with the ascent of the Law, but the effort is well worth it. From the summit, the route slips down into the historic and picturesque North Berwick.

This most agreeable and easy walk takes to the course of a once-popular railway, and links two attractive villages of some antiquity. The ambiance is delightful, the hedgerows loud with bird song.

Arguably the most exhilarating walk in the Pentlands, climbing energetically to an undulating ridge; a simple descent leads to the roadhead and an easy walk back to the start.

Tucked away on the northern slopes of the Lammermuir Hills, the lakes and woodlands of the Pressmennan Nature Reserve are a haven for wildlife and seldom visited by crowds.

A splendid, airy walk in the company of Faseny Water, before climbing onto Priestlaw Hill, with a splendid view. *The descent is across rough ground, so careful steps and navigation skills are necessary.*

At the heart of Scotland's central industrial belt, the country park that flanks the River Almond is an interlude of delight, a haven for wildlife that appreciates the richly wooded gorge.

The beautiful architectural detail of Roslin Chapel is the highlight of this walk, which earlier passes through a lovely wooded glen. The chapel featured in the film, *The Da Vinci Code*, starring Tom Hanks.

Climbing to the highest point of the Pentland Hills, and preceded by two lower but no less interesting hills, this walk offers outstanding views, *but does need to be reserved for days of good visibility.*

There are no taxing gradients along this peaceful reservoir walk, set against a fine backdrop of the Pentland Hills, Black Hill in particular, and there is constant interest on the water and in the woodlands.

Introduction to Edinburgh, Pentland Hills and the Lothians

Introduction to the Pentland Hills and the Lothians

There can be few cities in Britain or indeed elsewhere that have a finer setting than Edinburgh. Its position on the southern shores of the Firth of Forth – at the eastern end of the central lowland belt between the Highlands to the north and the Southern Uplands to the south – made it the ideal site for Scotland's capital, even though it did not attain that role until the 15th century.

The impressive landscape of the city was formed by geological action that occurred over aeons of time, Arthur's Seat and Castle Rock were both part of the Edinburgh Volcano which erupted 325 million years ago, forming Calton Hill. About this remarkable landscape is built a beautiful and fascinating city, renowned throughout the world for its heritage and architecture.

The area around Edinburgh, the Lothian region, has a fascinating mix of coastal panoramas and inspirational vistas. From Bass Rock and Berwick Law of North Berwick in East Lothian, through the Pentland Hills of Midlothian, to the historic royal burgh of Linlithgow in West Lothian, the region is rich in both terrain and heritage.

Priestlaw Hill

Dalmeny Shore, South Queensferry

Superb mixture of hills and lowland

Beyond the suburbs of Edinburgh lies ideal country for walking: a superb mixture of empty rolling hills, expansive moorland, delightful rivers, bounded by fertile lowlands, and an impressive coastline.

The hills begin almost in the centre of Edinburgh itself. When strolling down Princes Street, the impressive profile of Arthur's Seat dominates the skyline, rearing above Holyrood Park at the bottom end of the Royal Mile. The short, steep climb to its 823-foot (251m) summit provides magnificent panoramic views over the city, across the Firth of Forth, along a lengthy stretch of the Lothian coast and across the flattish terrain to the south of Edinburgh to the outlines of the nearest hills.

Nearest of all are the Pentlands, whose smooth, steep slopes extend in a roller-coaster fashion south-westwards from the southern outskirts of the city. Despite a maximum height of only 1,898 feet (579m), the abrupt manner in which they rise above the surrounding country gives them the appearance of a much more extensive mountain range. In reality they are a gem of a location for walkers, described by author Robert Louis Stevenson as 'the Hills of Home'. With a large number of waymarked and clearly signed paths, they provide unrivalled walking opportunities right on the doorstep of the Scottish capital. The broken range of the Pentland Hills begins roughly three miles south-west of Edinburgh and stretches some 16 miles into Lanarkshire. Views from the Pentland Ridge, and particularly from the summit Scald Law, are superb, taking in the Lammermuirs and the Firth of Forth.

Pressmennan Wood

Looking south-eastwards from the main Pentland ridge, the long, undulating lines of the Moorfoot and Lammermuir hills fill the horizon. The Lammermuirs are nearest the coast and create a broad wedge between the lowlands of East Lothian to the north and those of the Merse to the south. The Moorfoots present a steeper face and are more thickly forested, especially on their southern slopes, which descend to the Tweed valley.

The hills of the Scottish Borders are an obvious attraction for walkers, but the coast and the lowlands of East Lothian have plenty of attractions. There are fine, bracing walks along the rugged cliffs of the Berwickshire coast; farther north beyond Dunbar the coast becomes gentler, comprising a mixture of low cliffs, salt marshes and dunes. The lowlands themselves are not flat but undulating, interspersed with low hills and punctuated with sharp, dramatic-looking volcanic outcrops: North Berwick Law, Traprain Law and Bass Rock just off the coast, are all striking landmarks that can be seen for miles around. A delightful walk can be enjoyed in the valley of Whiteadder, while Lammer Law, one of the highest peaks of the Lammermuir Hills, provides a breezy upland challenge. East Lothian has always been one of the most fertile and prosperous agricultural regions of Scotland and this can be seen on the walks that take in the red-tiled villages of East Lothian and the handsome and dignified buildings of Haddington.

West Lothian is a region with both agricultural and industrial heritage, though the coal mining that once was so prevalent in the small towns and villages has gone. Linlithgow in the north has a strong history as an ancient burgh and a remarkable palace that sits beside the town's loch that makes a great attraction for visitors.

The walks in this book take advantage of variety in the terrain and landscape, and still manage to hold intrigue in one form or another in every walk; scratch the surface here and it bleeds history. The routes follow not only footpaths, but also a canal-side path, a disused railway line, and a sizeable chunk of the sand dune and low cliff coastline. And while there is nothing here equivalent to tackling Munros (although quite a few can be seen from the top of Allermuir Hill), the walking is for folk who enjoy less ambitious routes, imbued with just enough demands on skill and energy to make them exciting, they are significantly better compared with many Munros in their exquisite beauty and appeal. The hills of the Pentlands and the Lothians are simple of design, wide-eyed and beautiful.

This book includes a list of waypoints alongside the description of the walk, so that you can enjoy the full benefits of gps should you wish to. For more information on using your gps, read the *Pathfinder® Guide GPS for Walkers,* by gps teacher and navigation trainer, Clive Thomas (ISBN 978-0-7117-4445-5). For essential information on map reading and basic navigation, read the *Pathfinder® Guide Map Reading Skills* by outdoor writer, Terry Marsh (ISBN 978-0-7117-4978-8). Both titles are available in bookshops or can be ordered online at www.totalwalking.co.uk

Duddingston Loch and village from Queen's Drive, Holyrood Park, Edinburgh

Linlithgow Loch

		GPS waypoints
Start	Linlithgow	
Distance	2½ miles (4.2km)	✒ NT 002 772
Height gain	165 feet (50m)	Ⓐ NS 996 774
Approximate time	1 hour	Ⓑ NT 009 778
Parking	Linlithgow	Ⓒ NT 006 773
Route terrain	Surfaced paths around parkland	
Ordnance Survey maps	Landranger 65 (Falkirk & Linlithgow), Explorer 349 (Falkirk, Cumbernauld & Livingston)	

The highlights of this flat and easy circuit around Linlithgow Loch are the constantly changing views of Linlithgow Palace and St Michael's Church perched above the southern shores. From the north-east corner the views across the loch are enhanced by the distinctive shape of Cockleroy in the background. A springtime visit is invariably rewarded with a fine display of wild flowers and birdlife.

Two grand adjacent buildings dominate the old town of Linlithgow and all the views across the loch. The substantial ruins of Linlithgow Palace, popular residence of Stuart kings and birthplace in 1542 of Mary Queen of Scots, date from the 15th to the 17th centuries. James I of Scotland started building in 1425, and the work was completed around the middle of the 16th century. Extensions and repairs were carried out in the 17th century, but the palace became a ruin when it was carelessly set alight by some of the Duke of Cumberland's troops in 1746, following the Jacobite Rebellion. The church next to it, one of the finest in Scotland, dates from the 15th and 16th centuries, apart from the thin modern aluminium spire above the west tower.

✒ The walk starts at Linlithgow Cross in the town centre. Walk up Kirkgate towards the palace and through the gateway, and then immediately turn left down a surfaced path to the loch side.

Follow a tarmac path beside a picnic and play area, which later curves to the right along the west side of the loch. All the way there are superb views of the palace and church above the loch from a variety of angles. In the north-west corner, cross a footbridge Ⓐ and turn right at a fork to continue along the north shore of the loch, passing houses. The path along the north shore is a good place to look for wild flowers, among which you may find cotton thistle (the heraldic emblem of Scotland), hardheads, blue comfrey, meadow cranesbill, ragwort, speedwell, chickweed, wild strawberries and white dead nettle.

After passing the last of the houses, the tarmac path becomes a rough path, screened from the nearby M9 by a grassy and wooded embankment on the left, but the noise of the traffic is inescapable. This is a particularly

Linlithgow Palace from across the loch

Cross a footbridge and follow the tarmac path to the left to continue along the south side of the loch towards the palace and church. At a path junction below the palace ruins, turn left along an uphill path, later turning right to pass between the palace and church.

St Michael's Church is a magnificent building and worth exploring. Its stained glass windows are delightful and there are a number of Consecration Crosses carved into the walls, marking the places where the consecration water of Bishop de Bernham is said to have fallen at the time of the dedication of the original building in 1242.

Turn left through the palace gateway known as The Fore, built for James V around 1535 to give access to The Peel or outer enclosure of the palace, to return to the start. ●

attractive stretch of the walk, with superb views to the right of the palace with the prominent hill of Cockleroy beyond.

Just before emerging onto a lane, turn right **B** through a kissing-gate to follow a grassy path beside the east shores of the loch, bending right to continue along the south shore. The path later bears left away from the loch, beside woodland on the right, to go through a kissing-gate on to a road. Turn right and then at a sign 'Linlithgow Peel and Palace' turn right again **C** along a tarmac path between houses on the right and a church on the left, which heads downhill to rejoin the loch shore.

0	200	400	600	800 METRES	1	
						KILOMETRES
						MILES
0	200	400	600 YARDS	½		

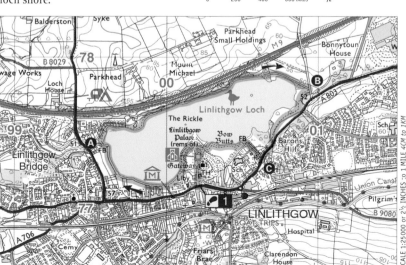

SCALE 1:25000 or 2½ INCHES to 1 MILE 4CM to 1KM

Dunbar and Belhaven Bay

		GPS waypoints
Start	Dunbar harbour	
Distance	2½ miles (4.7km)	☑ NT 679 791
Height gain	275 feet (85m)	Ⓐ NT 676 792
Approximate time	1½ hours	Ⓑ NT 662 786
Parking	Dunbar Leisure Pool	
Route terrain	Paved coastal path; road walking	
Ordnance Survey maps	Landranger 67 (Duns, Dunbar & Eyemouth), Explorer 351 (Dunbar & North Berwick)	

With fine sandy beaches and an attractive location, Dunbar has become a popular seaside resort, but it is also an historic town. Of the once great castle – one of the most important medieval fortresses in Scotland – only a few crumbling walls survive above the harbour, but the High Street contains the imposing 17th-century Town House and the birthplace of John Muir, now a museum. Muir was born in 1838, emigrated to America with his family at the age of 11 and later played a major role in the creation of the Yosemite and other National Parks. The present short and relaxing walk serves as a taster for the trail, and follows a lovely route along the cliffs from Dunbar Harbour to Belhaven Bay, before returning to the town by way of a quiet road.

🖊 Walk down to Victoria Harbour and turn left to make your way towards

Dunbar Castle

the fragmentary ruins of the castle at its west end. Just before reaching them, turn left onto a surfaced path leading up to the Dunbar Leisure Pool, where

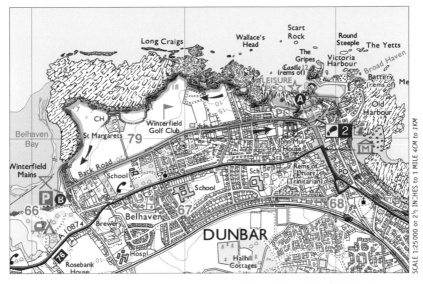

the John Muir Way is signposted. The Way extends for almost 45 miles, linking East Lothian with Edinburgh and the Scottish Borders.

Pass in front of the leisure pool, and then to the rear of an ancillary building to reach a signpost at the top of a flight of steps **A** taking you down to the rocky shoreline. On your right are some of the rock pools where the young Muir 'loved to wander ... and wonder at the shells and seaweeds, eels and crabs' he discovered at low tide. In the early 20th century, this area was an open-air swimming pool, which continued to operate until the present pool was built in the 1980s.

Go down the steps, and follow a brief but mildly convoluted pathway at the water's edge, crossing the base of another, walled flight of steps. About 50 yds farther on, turn acutely left, climbing steps and soon passing through a narrow tunnel, and forward along a path that finally hauls up to the war memorial.

Turn right here onto a paved esplanade that twists and turns above the rocky coast, giving fine retrospective views of Dunbar Castle,

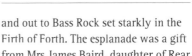

and out to Bass Rock set starkly in the Firth of Forth. The esplanade was a gift from Mrs James Baird, daughter of Rear Admiral Hay of Belton, and it is every bit as agreeable as it no doubt was when constructed in 1893.

As you walk on along the esplanade, sandwiched between a wall and sea cliffs, so eventually the expanse of Belhaven Bay comes into view, backed by long golden sands and the distant lump of Traprain Law. At the end of the wall, the path turns left to pass below Winterfield Golf Course, descending sleeper steps, which are slippery when wet. The ongoing path passes along the shoreline, occasionally touching on golf course tees, and finally leading round to a car park at the end of a lane, near a group of wooden chalets.

Continue across the car park and then turn left at a signpost for the John Muir Way. Head along a lane and, just after passing the Shore Road car park, turn left **B** onto Back Road (signed for the town centre), and follow this back to the start.   ●

Pressmennan Wood and Lake

		GPS waypoints
Start	Pressmennan Lake	
Distance	3 miles (4.8km)	NT 622 726
Height gain	605 feet (185m)	**Ⓐ** NT 621 726
Approximate time	1½ hours	**Ⓑ** NT 631 732
Parking	The Woodland Trust car park at the	**Ⓒ** NT 636 734
	west end of Pressmennan Lake.	**Ⓓ** NT 634 734
	From Stenton, take the lane	**Ⓔ** NT 629 729
	signposted to Deuchrie and, just after Rucklaw West	
	Mains Farm, turn left onto a track at a 'Forest Trail	
	Car Park' sign	
Route terrain	Mainly forest trails and paths	
Ordnance Survey maps	Landranger 67 (Duns, Dunbar & Eyemouth),	
	Explorer 351 (Dunbar & North Berwick)	

The Woodland Trust owns 210 acres of land on the south side of Pressmennan Lake, which lies south west of Dunbar. The narrow lake is man-made and the trees are mixed, deciduous predominating. The walk follows the shore of the lake on the outward section, but returns on a higher path giving extensive views over East Lothian and beyond.

Return to the entrance to the car park and head back down the track to find a path on the right, which soon reaches a track. Turn sharply right again to take a path running beside a tiny burn. It soon reaches Pressmennan Lake **Ⓐ**, a narrow man-made stretch of water surrounded by magnificent trees. Note the wild raspberries, which grow here. Nearby Stenton is noted for its soft fruit and birds have seeded the canes here. The twisting lakeside path, which must once have been choked by rhododendrons, reveals a succession of vistas.

The path climbs to run by the edge of replanted woodland and then meanders among trees before climbing again to reach a seat carved from a tree where it joins a track **Ⓑ**.

Bear left along the track and pass a fallen beech tree, which has been skilfully chainsawed into the form of a seat. At the end of the lake **Ⓒ** steps take a path down to the dam. Walk across this and then take the grassy path away from the lake. This can be boggy in places.

Bear right before a gate leading into a field to follow the track, which makes a sweeping right-hand turn and begins to climb. It proves to be the track left earlier for the dam. About 250 yds past the steps, look for a path on the left **Ⓓ** that climbs through the trees giving ever more spectacular views

Pressmennan Wood

northwards. These are at their best when the path reaches the top of the wood. North Berwick Law and Bass Rock are clearly visible. Wild flowers are abundant with honeysuckle climbing the trunks of many trees. Too soon the path reaches a wide grassy picnic area **E**, which provides a final chance to view the surrounding countryside. From here a track leads back through trees to the car park. ●

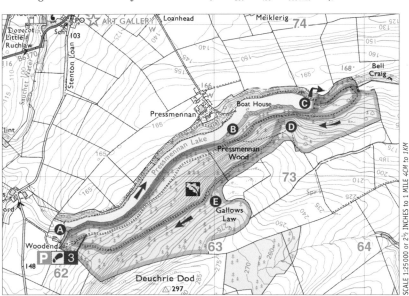

Threipmuir and Harlaw Reservoirs

		GPS waypoints
Start	Threipmuir Reservoir	☑ NT 166 639
Distance	3½ miles (5.5km)	Ⓐ NT 178 643
Height gain	130 feet (40m)	Ⓑ NT 181 652
Approximate time	1½ hours	Ⓒ NT 176 644
Parking	Threipmuir car park on the left of the road running south from Balerno	
Route terrain	Reservoir paths; woodland	
Ordnance Survey maps	Landranger 65 (Falkirk & Linlithgow), Explorer 344 (Pentland Hills)	

Besides being a lovely stroll along the shores of two man-made lakes, this walk also serves to give the newcomer an understanding of the geography of the Pentland Hills. Bird-lovers will find a variety of species both on the water and in the woodlands that fringe the reservoirs.

☑ From the car park go past the noticeboard and turn left along a track signposted to Harlaw. Keep ahead at the gate where the drive on the right goes to Easter Bavelaw, the farm on the other side of Threipmuir Reservoir. Once by the shoreline the track runs in a straight line relatively close to the water. There

Harlaw Reservoir

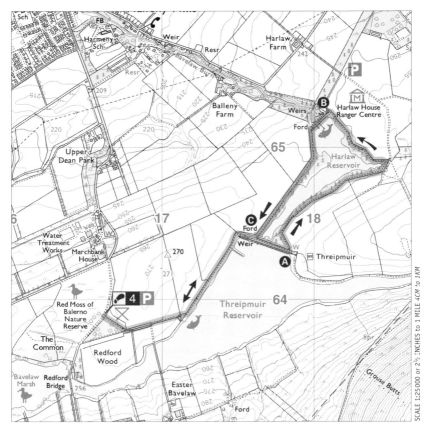

SCALE 1:25000 or 2½ INCHES to 1 MILE 4CM to 1KM

are sandy beaches by a rocky jetty at the northern end of the reservoir, which are popular as paddling and bathing places. Turn right, cross the dam and then go through a kissing-gate on the left Ⓐ to walk by the side of Harlaw Reservoir.

This smaller reservoir has more trees around it though you have to be aware of cyclists who also use the narrow path, made rough by exposed tree roots. The scent of resin from the pine trees on a hot day is a memorable feature of the walk. The view north-eastwards to Allermuir Hill reveals typical Pentlands scenery.

Harlaw and Threipmuir reservoirs were built between 1848 and 1890 to maintain a reliable supply of water for the Edinburgh water-powered mills, which had previously relied solely on

the Water of Leith. Today, all the industry has gone, but the reservoirs are enjoying a new lease of life as sanctuaries for wildlife and for informal recreation.

Turn left at the overflow channel Ⓑ to walk on a broad track along the western shore of Harlaw Reservoir, which is also fringed with pine trees.

Rejoin the outward route at Threipmuir dam Ⓒ to return to the car park. The view of the Pentland Hills is stunning, with Scald Law and Black Hill easily identifiable. You may well spot a great crested grebe or a pair of teal on the water – both breed here though their favourite sites are at Bavelaw Marsh, at the very western end of the reservoir. ●

Caerketton Hill

Start	Boghall Farm	GPS waypoints
Distance	3 miles (5km)	🥾 NT 245 652
Height gain	1,000 feet (305m)	Ⓐ NT 242 652
		Ⓑ NT 232 663
Approximate time	2 hours	Ⓒ NT 241 661
Parking	At start	Ⓓ NT 244 662
Route terrain	Mountain slopes; farmland	
Ordnance Survey maps	Landranger 66 (Edinburgh), Explorer 344 (Pentland Hills)	

Brief as it may seem, this delightful circuit not only gives an introduction to walking in the Pentlands, but also provides a stunning view of Edinburgh, the Firth of Forth and beyond. The walking is excellent throughout, and well worth the effort. That the walk may be extended to include Allermuir Hill (otherwise visited in Walk 17) is a bonus.

🥾 Begin from the car park at Boghall Farm by walking through a gate in a corner to gain an enclosed path that wends a way around the farm, finally emerging at a broad track. Turn right and walk up as far as a cottage Ⓐ. Here the track divides. Keep left, passing sheep pens and walk on through a gate and onto a vehicle track heading up Boghall Glen. In the upper part of the glen the terrain changes noticeably to rough grazing, where hardy black-faced sheep roam the hillsides, and red grouse breed in the heather.

The track climbs easily into the glen, but later levels off for a while, running forward to a gate and stile. For a while, beyond the gate, the track continues more or less horizontally, but then starts climbing again to another gate and stile. The rounded summit directly in front of you is Allermuir Hill.

Keep following the track, aiming eventually for a pair of ladder-stiles.

Cross both stiles, and, a short way on, when the ongoing path forks, keep left. Gradually the path works a way round to another stile below Windy Door Nick Ⓑ, a neat gap (bealach) between Caerketton Hill and Allermuir Hill. It is also aptly named, more often than not. *This is the point where, if you intend including Allermuir Hill, you will bear left, crossing the bealach east-to-west and then climbing steeply, but briefly, to the top of Allermuir Hill, and then retracing your steps.*

Otherwise, turn right and head for Caerketton Hill, first reaching a large pile of stones on Caerketton Craigs. There is some suggestion that the cairn is of Bronze Age origin, it is certainly a Scheduled Ancient Monument. Continue across the summit, following a fence line to reach Caerketton Hill Ⓒ. The view from these summits, minor as they may be in the scale of things, was one much admired by Robert Louis Stevenson, who spent time at the village of Swanston to the north, and set one of his novels there. He ended his years far away on the Pacific island of Samoa, longing for what he described as his 'Hills of Home'.

From Caerketton Hill, the path descends very steeply. When it swings left to head towards the top of the Midlothian Artificial Ski Slope, leave it, and continue to descend steeply beside a fence. At the bottom of the first stage of the descent **D**, cross a stile and turn right onto a path for Boghall Farm.

Follow a grassy path, and when it divides, keep alongside the adjacent fence, descending steeply once more through banks of gorse and bracken. At the bottom of the descent, cross another stile, continuing in the direction of Boghall. The path, seasonally overgrown, leads to a stile spanning a fence. Over this keep descending the hillside, obliquely,

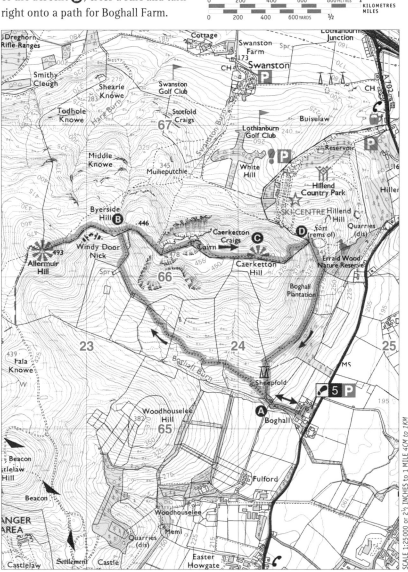

staying roughly parallel with a fence on the left, to go down to a kissing-gate. Ignore the gate and keep on down beside the fence, closely pressed beside it by gorse. At the bottom, turn left through another gate descending a field edge towards the Boghall car park, and soon reach the cottage passed earlier in the walk Ⓐ. Bear left, retracing your steps to the start. ●

Caerketton Hill

Arthur's Seat

		GPS waypoints
Start	Palace of Holyroodhouse, Edinburgh	✐ NT 271 737
Distance	3½ miles (5.5km)	Ⓐ NT 275 736
Height gain	1,080 feet (330m)	Ⓑ NT 275 729
		Ⓒ NT 283 726
Approximate time	2 hours	Ⓓ NT 274 724
Parking	Car park just beyond entrance to palace	Ⓔ NT 272 728
Route terrain	Managed paths; parkland; some road walking; rocky hill top	
Ordnance Survey maps	Landranger 66 (Edinburgh), Explorer 350 (Edinburgh)	

There is a ruggedness and sense of remoteness on parts of this walk in Holyrood Park that makes it difficult to believe that you are within the city boundaries of Edinburgh, scarcely a stone's throw from the bustle of Princes Street. Despite its modest height of 823 feet (251m), the climb up to Arthur's Seat is quite steep and exhausting, and it may well be one of the most frequently ascended hills in Britain. The view from the top surpasses that of many higher peaks, stretching right across Lowland Scotland and along the Lothian coast. After descending, the route continues by way of the village of Duddingston and beside Duddingston Loch. The final section over Salisbury Crags gives particularly dramatic views of the irregular jumble of buildings and spires that create the picturesque skyline of Scotland's capital.

The Palace of Holyroodhouse at the bottom end of Edinburgh's Royal Mile began life as the guest house of Holyrood Abbey, substantial portions of which survive on its north side. James IV began it in 1501, but most of the present building dates from the late 17th century when Charles II rebuilt it following destruction. Holyrood Park was originally the park attached to the palace. With the steep, rocky, volcanic slopes of Arthur's Seat and the three lochs around its base, it gives the impression that a piece of the Highlands has been transported to the suburbs of Edinburgh.

✐ Begin by crossing the road from the car park into the park and turning left along a gently ascending tarmac track. St Margaret's Loch is soon seen ahead. The track curves right. At a fork, take the left-hand path that descends slightly into the flat, grassy valley known as Dry Dam or Long Row. On the hill ahead are the scanty ruins of St Anthony's Chapel, overlooking the loch.

Bear right **A** along a clear, grassy path for the ascent of Arthur's Seat. At first the path climbs steadily through the valley, making directly for the blunt, prominent bulk of Arthur's Seat; later the going becomes steeper. Follow the path as it veers left, climbs a series of steps, then continue ignoring all turn-offs until you reach the one that turns sharp right to ascend to the summit beside a chain link fence. Keep on this well-paved path to the triangulation pillar and view indicator **B**. From here you have grand views along the Firth of Forth to the coasts of Lothian and Fife. Closer to hand is the Old Town dominated at one end by Edinburgh Castle and at the other by the Palace of Holyrood and the award-winning design of the Scottish Parliament building.

Dunsapie Loch

Start the descent by retracing your steps to where the path bends sharply to the left. Here leave the outward route by keeping ahead in the direction of Dunsapie Loch below, descending easily along a broad, smooth, grassy path to reach the road that encircles the park, opposite a car park and just to the right of the loch. Cross the road and, in the right-hand corner of the car park, turn right along a path that skirts the base of the hill on the left. At a fork, take the

Arthur's Seat and Edinburgh from Allermuir Hill

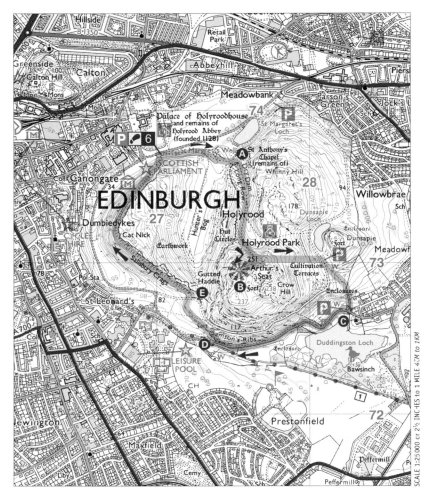

SCALE 1:25 000 or 2½ INCHES to 1 MILE 4CM to 1KM

right-hand path downhill towards a wall, turn right alongside the wall and descend a long flight of steps to a road **C**. *If you wish to visit Duddingston village – a rural enclave with a 12th-century church perched above the loch – turn left.* Otherwise, turn right along the winding road above Duddingston Loch on the left and later below the almost perpendicular, rocky, gorse-covered slopes of Samson's Ribs on the right.

Bear right off the road **D** along a grassy path to follow the base of the slopes as they bear right, heading gently uphill towards the prominent jagged outlines of Salisbury Crags, to reach the

park circular road again. Turn right for a few strides and, where the road bends right, turn sharp left **E** onto a stony track that heads steadily uphill, flattens out and then descends quite steeply across the face of Salisbury Crags. This is the Radical Road, constructed in the 1820s, allegedly to provide work for the unemployed, and from it there are superb views to the left across Edinburgh.

The track reaches the circular road opposite the car park and starting point of the walk.

Hailes Castle

		GPS waypoints
Start	East Linton	
Distance	3¾ miles (6km)	NT 591 774
Height gain	310 feet (95m)	Ⓐ NT 576 760
Approximate time	2 hours	Ⓑ NT 593 770
Parking	Smiddy Wynd, Stories Park	
Route terrain	Riverside path; country lane	
Ordnance Survey maps	Landranger 67 (Duns, Dunbar & Eyemouth), Explorer 351 (Dunbar & North Berwick)	

A pleasant footpath along the banks of the River Tyne leads from East Linton to the attractively sited ruins of Hailes Castle. From here the walk returns directly to East Linton along a quiet lane high above the river.

Walk down the main street in East Linton to a T-junction. Turn right, passing beneath a railway bridge, and a few strides farther on turn sharp left at a 'Public Path for Hailes Castle' sign, following a descending track that heads

Hailes Castle

down to the river. Turn right at the bottom onto the riverside path.

Pass beneath the A199 to continue along this most attractive, narrow path beside the River Tyne. Part of the route is through woodland. At one stage you climb steps above the river – from where there is a lovely view of the Tyne

below and Traprain Law in the background – later descending steps to rejoin the riverbank, to continue along the edge of sloping meadows.

Climb a stile to walk through more trees, passing below a sheer cliff-face to reach a footbridge by Hailes Mill **A**. Turn left over it and follow the uphill path ahead to a lane. Keep ahead along the lane to the remains of the mainly 13th-century Hailes Castle.

Hailes Castle, formerly the seat of the earls of Bothwell, occupies a fine position above the river. Mary Queen of Scots stayed here in 1567 as the new wife of James Hepburn, Earl of Bothwell; he was her third husband and one of the conspirators involved in the murder of her second husband, Darnley. The castle was originally founded in the 12th century as a fortified tower house by Hugo de Gourlay, one of the oldest buildings of its kind in Scotland. It served chiefly as a private house, but also formed the focal point of the lord's estate. The castle did not figure in any major siege, but it was attacked from time to time. In 1446, the pro-English Archibald of Dunbar stormed the castle, killing everyone therein. Oliver Cromwell's army is said to have dismantled the castle in 1650. Supporting the English in the Scottish Wars of Independence, proved to be an action for which the Gourlays forfeited their lands.

On leaving the castle, which is managed by Historic Scotland and open free of charge at all reasonable hours, turn left and walk back along the lane, continuing all the way to East Linton, an easy and enjoyable experience. On arriving at East Linton you pass beneath the railway line again **B**. Turn left, cross the Tyne bridge, and right into the main street to complete the walk. ●

SCALE 1:25 000 or 2½ INCHES to 1 MILE 4CM to 1KM

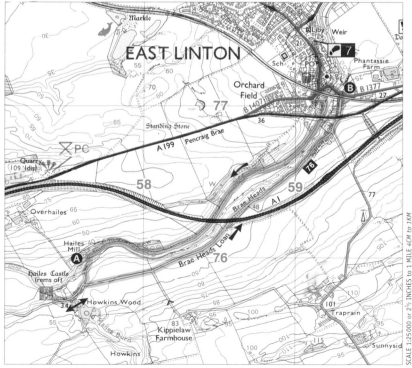

Roslin Glen Country Park

		GPS waypoints
Start	Roslin Glen	
Distance	3¾ miles (6km)	✎ NT 273 628
Height gain	490 feet (150m)	Ⓐ NT 275 628
		Ⓑ NT 286 644
Approximate time	2 hours	Ⓒ NT 272 632
Parking	At start	
Route terrain	Semi-urban parkland; woodland; minor roads	
Ordnance Survey maps	Landranger 66 (Edinburgh), Explorer 344 (Pentland Hills)	

Below the village of Roslin, the River North Esk flows through a dramatic, narrow, steep-sided and thickly wooded glen, part of which is now a country park. The first half of the walk follows an undulating path through the glen, and the return leg is along a track and lane above it. Near the end you pass Roslin Chapel, one of the most fascinating buildings in Scotland. This featured in Dan Brown's novel The Da Vinci Code *and scenes for the film of the same name starring Tom Hanks were shot here in 2005.*

✎ From the car park, start by taking the path to the river, walking through light woodland cover to reach the riverbank at a footbridge. Cross the bridge, which spans the North Esk, and continue along an uphill path through woodland. At the bottom of a flight of steps, turn right Ⓐ to pass beneath the bridge that (above you) leads to the sparse remains of the medieval Roslin Castle, largely destroyed by the English armies of Henry VIII in 1544, partially restored in the early 17th century and destroyed again by the English, this time under Oliver Cromwell, in 1650.

Descend via shallow steps and turn left to start the walk through the thickly wooded glen. This is a superb walk through beautiful woodland, carpeted with bluebells in spring, and at times the cliffs on both sides of the glen are virtually perpendicular. After passing through a gap in a fence, you initially climb above the glen to reach a crossing of paths near the top edge of the woodland. Turn right here along a path that descends steeply, zigzagging in places, to the bottom of the glen and turn left to continue by the river. Later the path heads quite steeply uphill to a stile. Climb it and continue along the top of the glen. There is a fine view through the trees on the right of the mainly 17th-century Hawthornden Castle on the other side of the gorge. After a while the path descends again to continue just above the river, with more open views to the left across fields.

Soon after climbing a stile, you emerge from the wooded glen and follow the river round a right-hand bend to a kissing-gate. Turn left away from the river along Hewan Bog boundary fence to a steep uphill path

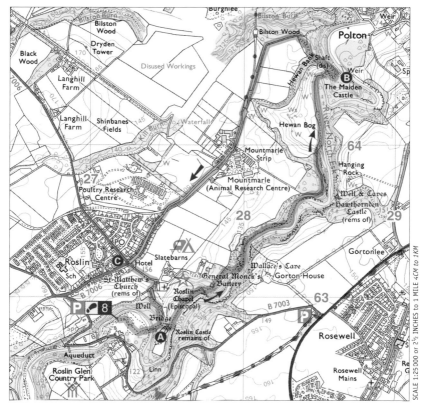

with steps leading to a plateau **B**. From here there are fine views of Roslin Glen on the left and Bilston Glen on the right. At a fork keep left and continue to another kissing-gate that leads to a track on the edge of woodland.

Turn left along the track that keeps along the edge of woodland, curving left. Later come fine views to the right of the Pentland Hills. Go through a gate and continue along a tarmac farm track – later a lane – into Roslin. Bear left to cross a bridge over a disused railway and continue through the village to a crossroads **C**.

Turn left, and ahead is Roslin Chapel, which overlooks the glen. It was built in the 15th century by Henry Sinclair, Earl of Orkney, as a large collegiate church but only the choir was ever completed. The chapel is unusually flamboyant for a later medieval Scottish church,

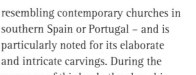

resembling contemporary churches in southern Spain or Portugal – and is particularly noted for its elaborate and intricate carvings. During the currency of this book, the chapel is undergoing extensive renovation for a four-year period from 2009, although it remains substantially open (admission charge).

Just before reaching the chapel, the route turns right, in the direction of the 'castle', downhill along a tarmac track. At a footpath sign for Polton, turn left along a walled track that bears right downhill back into the wooded glen. In front of a metal gate by the castle, head down a flight of steps on the right to rejoin the outward route and retrace your steps to the start. ●

North Berwick Law

		GPS waypoints
Start	North Berwick	
Distance	3¾ miles (6km)	✎ NT 553 842
Height gain	675 feet (205m)	Ⓐ NT 553 840
		Ⓑ NT 559 845
Approximate time	2 hours	Ⓒ NT 561 847
Parking	Car park on west side of hill off	Ⓓ NT 554 855
	B1347	Ⓔ NT 553 852
Route terrain	Tracks and steep paths; exposed summit; road walking	
Ordnance Survey maps	Landrangers 66 (Edinburgh) and 67 (Duns, Dunbar & Eyemouth), Explorer 351 (Dunbar & North Berwick)	

The Law can be seen as a landmark from many of the other summits featured in this book and is, like Arthur's Seat and Bass Rock, the core of an ancient volcano. It is the finest viewpoint along the East Lothian coast and a clear day is essential for the climb. The rest of the walk may seem a little of an anti-climax, but there is plenty of interest in the buildings of the town while the shady Glen contrasts well with the open countryside seen earlier. North Berwick Law suffers from fragile soil so it is as well to obey the advice given on the plaque at the start to stay on the waymarked paths (though these may be hard to spot in places).

✎ The path initially skirts a wood as it swings around the south side of the Law beneath low cliffs. The letters 'GBH' are painted in white at the end of these and having passed this point Ⓐ the clearly defined grassy path becomes very steep for a short distance. Then it bends right to make a more gradual ascent. Tantallon Castle comes into view ahead and then the path begins to zigzag. Within half an hour of leaving the car park you should be at the top of the Law where there is an ancient whalebone, a triangulation pillar, and a viewpoint indicator. There is evidence of human occupation on the hill dating from the Iron Age, and possibly extending into the Middle Ages.

Retrace your steps from the summit until you catch sight of the pond on the western side of the Law. You will first pass a white bench and then a white seat. The path gradually swings northwards and the tower of a disused windmill lies ahead. You may see wild goats grazing on the hillside among the sheep.

At the bottom of the Law Ⓐ bear left on a sheep track just above the fence. This gradually swings round to give views towards the town. Looking in this direction you will see a gate Ⓑ in a wall in the front of houses. Make for this by zigzagging down to the lower ground taking care to skirt the dense whin and avoid boggy patches.

Go through the kissing-gate and turn right at the road. Pass the entrance to a supermarket and turn right at the main road. Cross the road to take a path **C** waymarked to 'The Glen'. This follows a small burn with a playing field to the left at first. Then it plunges into more dense woodland and continues to follow the course of the burn, emerging into the open by a golf clubhouse. Turn left at the shore and follow the road round to the harbour.

Turn sharp left at the Lifeboat Station **D** towards the Law to pass the Baptist chapel and go down Quality Street to the tourist information centre. Pass this and bear right at Kirk Pots passing the romantic ruins of St Andrew's Church. Beyond this turn left following the sign

North Berwick Law

to North Berwick Law **E**. Climb the hill and pass the sports centre and school to keep ahead when the main road sweeps right and thus reach the car park. ●

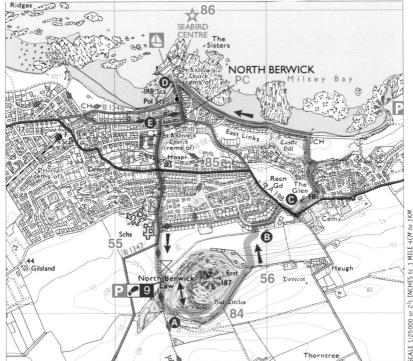

Beecraigs and Cockleroy

		GPS waypoints
Start	Beecraigs Country Park	🖉 NT 007 746
Distance	4½ miles (7.2km)	Ⓐ NT 010 744
Height gain	575 feet (175m)	Ⓑ NT 008 739
Approximate time	2½ hours	Ⓒ NS 998 736
Parking	At start	Ⓓ NS 993 742
Route terrain	Mainly managed parkland; upland paths	Ⓔ NS 998 741
Ordnance Survey maps	Landranger 65 (Falkirk & Linlithgow), Explorer 349 (Falkirk, Cumbernauld & Livingston)	

Beecraigs Country Park crams a diverse range of activities into its 913 acres. Human occupations cover a wide range of open-air pursuits from archery to orienteering, and there is also room for commercial deer and fish farms. The route goes through the mature woodlands of the park to Cockleroy Hill, which though of modest height, 912 feet (278m), is one of the finest viewpoints of lowland Scotland.

🖉 From the car park go over the bridge into the deer farm; there is a distant view of the Forth bridges. Pigs are kept in enclosures here as well as deer, which seem indifferent to visitors, even inquisitive children. Continue along a broad fence-lined path that turns sharp right then goes through a gate and into woodland to reach Beecraigs Loch Ⓐ.

Beecraigs Loch is a long-established loch where brown trout fishing first took place in 1922. In recent times, the best brown trout caught was a fish of 8lbs 5oz, but these days the loch is stocked with rainbow trout from a nearby farm. The paths are flanked by a lovely rash of wild flowers including self heal, meadow cranesbill, speedwell, ox-eye daisy, rosebay and broad-leaved willow herb.

Turn left and follow the shoreline in a clockwise direction. Bear right following a waymark to walk along the dam wall before going down steps opposite the trout farm, used as an educational resource. Climb the track away from the fish farm to pass the anglers' lodge and continue around the perimeter of the loch.

Opposite the island and immediately after crossing a bridge, turn left onto a footpath and follow red waymarks through the wood crossing in turn a bridge then a road Ⓑ to reach a signpost to Balvormie. From here continue on the path crossing another bridge and eventually reaching a T-junction. Turn left then immediately fork right and continue following waymarks to reach a crossroads with a fingerpost sign. Turn left. Do not cross the bridge, but keep ahead to cross another bridge a little way downstream. There are dense trees to the right and a wall to the left. Cross over a forest track

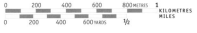

to another on the other side and keep ahead following the wall when this becomes a path used by ponies. At the road **C**, turn right and cross it to a metal gate with a gap on the left. Go through this to walk on a track with Balvormie Meadow on the right.

Turn right at a T-junction following a fingerpost pointing to Balvormie and then bear left on a track into the forest. Turn right at the next T-junction to arrive at a small circular clearing. Cross this to a path opposite that goes over a plank causeway and then climbs to meet another path. At the top turn sharp left and then right on to a short muddy track leading to another T-junction. Turn right here and then, after a few

strides, left on a path descending through trees to a plank causeway. After this climb a slight gradient and bear left to reach the road **D**.

Cross the road and keep ahead by the car park on a forest track which climbs beside a wall. Climb the stile on the right and the grassy slope to the summit of Cockleroy Hill marked by a triangulation pillar and indicator. The view extends from Bass Rock in the east to Goat Fell on the Isle of Arran to the west; Ben Vorlich and Ben More are two of the Trossach summits that can be identified.

Return to the stile and keep ahead on

the blue waymarked route to return to the road. Cross the road **D**, and bear right to retrace steps over the causeway. Keep ahead to pass toilets and come to the picnic area and pond **E**. Go across the road and through the car park to find the red and dark blue waymarks at the southern end.

A broad, well-surfaced path descends gently. Keep ahead on the red path when the blue branches to the right. A gate faces you when you reach the road.

Turn left before the gate and cross a footbridge to reach the Lochside car park. Cross the road here and follow red waymarks around the west shore of the loch crossing a plank causeway. Continue walking through the trees and at a second causeway (which has a wheelchair ramp) turn left to return on the path through the deer farm to the Park Centre. ●

The stunning view from Cockleroy Hill

Carlops and North Esk Reservoir

Start	Carlops	**GPS waypoints**	
Distance	4½ miles (7km)	✐ NT 161 559	
Height gain	835 feet (255m)	Ⓐ NT 154 578	
		Ⓑ NT 162 577	
Approximate time	2½ hours	Ⓒ NT 169 576	
Parking	At start	Ⓓ NT 167 567	
Route terrain	Upland moorland; farm track		
Ordnance Survey maps	Landranger 65 (Falkirk & Linlithgow), Explorer 344 (Pentland Hills)		

There is a charming aimlessness about this walk: not that you have no objective, but just that the pleasure of a gentle wander among the curvy Pentlands is most agreeable. This is a fine excuse for a half-day's potter around the hills; it should deter no one, and such ascents as there are, soon pass underfoot.

✐ Leave the car park opposite the parish church and walk up the minor road (signed for 'Buteland by the Borestane').

North Esk Reservoir in the folds of the Pentlands

When the surfaced lane swings left to Carlop Hill Farm, keep forward on a broad stony track heading into the lush folds of the Pentlands, a sudden and most agreeable transformation.

Heading for Carlops

the other side cross another stile and climb left to a signpost (Nine Mile Burn), and there turn right, climbing steeply. When the path forks, take the higher of the two. At a small rock, the path levels for a while and goes forward through bracken beyond which it starts to climb again. When it divides, branch left (waymark set in rock).

The track goes through a gate and round to pass Fairliehope Farm, beyond which it ascends gently to pass a small plantation of mixed woodland, where the ascent finally ends. Now North Esk Reservoir is in view.

The track then winds round to reach the waterman's cottage at the reservoir **A**. Just before the buildings take to a signposted route around them, which finally uses a stile to gain access to the dam.

The North Esk Reservoir, which has a surface area of 15.7 acres and holds 45 million gallons of water, was completed in 1850. It acted as a storage tank for the mills that operated on the River North Esk in the 19th and early 20th centuries, and maintained a constant flow in the river even during summer droughts, allowing manufacturing to continue throughout the year. The chief beneficiaries of this steady supply were the paper mills at Valleyfield Mill, Esk Mill and Bank Mill, which produced, as its name suggests, the paper for bank notes.

Walk across the dam and on

The path climbs to a bealach (col) between hills **B**, providing here the last opportunity to gaze back on the valley of the North Esk. Continue forward to meet and follow a fence to a gate. Beyond the gate a broad hill track leads down beside a wall, with the long low range of the Moorfoot and Lammermuir Hills in view in the far distance.

Go down through another gate and continue with the descending track towards Spittal Farm **C**. The route passes to the left of the farm, locates a kissing-gate and drops to a stony track to meet the farm access. Turn left, and follow the track out from Spittal Farm

Carlops parish church

to meet the quiet back road linking Nine Mile Burn with Carlops. Turn right on this, and follow it for about ½ mile. Then, just before the road turns left to go down to meet the A702, leave it by turning right at Wanton Wa's **D**, onto a minor road.

When the road surfacing ends and the ongoing track swings to the right, leave it on the apex by going forward onto a footpath signposted for Carlops. The path is seasonally overgrown with unclear edges, and fights its way through bracken, although speedwell, ragwort, willowherb, dog rose and foxglove manage to put in a colourful appearance.

A few steps finally bring the path down to meet the road, which is followed over Carlops Bridge back to the start. ●

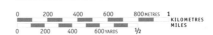

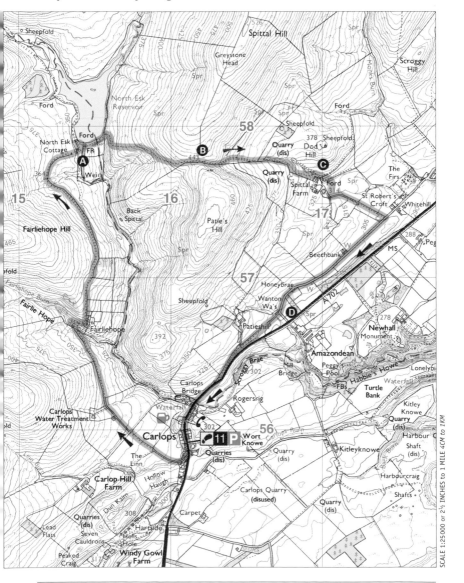

Gamelshiel Castle and Whiteadder Water

Gamelshiel Castle and Whiteadder Water

		GPS waypoints
Start	Western end of Whiteadder Reservoir	
Distance	4½ miles (7km)	
Height gain	855 feet (260m)	
Approximate time	2½ hours	
Parking	Small car park on left after crossing bridge at western end of Whiteadder Reservoir	
Route terrain	Rough mountain moorland	
Ordnance Survey maps	Landranger 67 (Duns, Dunbar & Eyemouth), Explorer 345 (Lammermuir Hills)	

GPS waypoints
- NT 646 642
- Ⓐ NT 645 646
- Ⓑ NT 649 648
- Ⓒ NT 642 671
- Ⓓ NT 638 657

Only two walls remain of Gamelshiel Castle, which stands in a remote position below Spartleton Hill in the Lammermuirs. Although little is known of its history, its stones speak eloquently of centuries of hardship and suffering. After the castle the route follows a track that strikes northwards across lonely moorland. The return is via the The Herring Road, a footpath close to the delightful Whiteadder Water.

The road between Gifford and Duns (B6355) crosses the northern arm of the Whiteadder Reservoir over a causeway and at the eastern end of the latter there is a small car park and a gate across a track which heads north.

Walk up this track to a sheepfold (marked as Sheep Wash on the map). Fork right here Ⓐ to follow the Hall Burn up to the castle Ⓑ whose crumbling walls frame a typical view of the Lammermuirs with Mayshiel Farm in the distance.

Not surprisingly, the castle is a Scheduled Ancient Monument, and believed to be a simple tower house dating from the 14th century.

The energetic will be tempted to climb to the

The crumbling walls of Gamelshiel Castle

summit of Spartleton Hill from this point, but *be warned, it is a stiff climb over rough ground from here and is better approached from Gamelshiel Farm to the east.* Our route fords Hall Burn (wearers of shorts should be warned that the castle is surrounded by nettlebeds) and then takes a footpath northwards which gradually climbs the western flank of Spartleton Hill. The walking is good on the grassy path, which runs just below the line where heather and bracken take over.

Beyond the top of Watch Cleugh the path becomes less clear. Fork right here to pass through a line of butts, and continue to head towards electric lines when a fence is joined to the right. Pass beneath the lines and keep walking ahead on a good track to reach a fence and then join The Herring Road.

Turn left here **C** to pass beneath the cables again and descend on the track, which goes round a sharp hairpin near the bottom. Before the gate leave the track **D** by turning left to cross Writerspath Burn and take a beautiful grassy track on the left bank of Whiteadder Water. There is a wonderful choice of places to picnic or paddle and the marshy ground near the head of the reservoir is the habitat of many unusual plants. All too

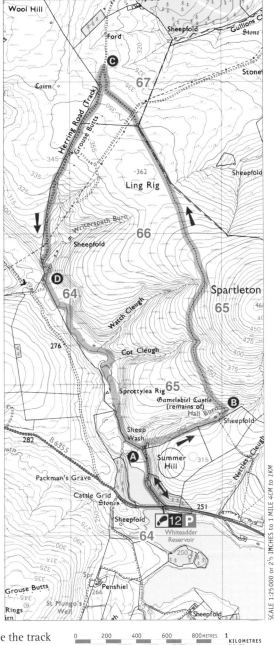

soon the sheepfold encountered at the start of the walk comes into view **A**.

Retrace your steps from here on the track, which returns to the little car park.

Monks Rig and West Kip

			GPS waypoints
Start	Nine Mile Burn		✒ NT 177 577
Distance	4½ miles (7km)		**Ⓐ** NT 174 583
Height gain	1,165 feet (355m)		**Ⓑ** NT 175 598
Approximate time	2½ hours		**Ⓒ** NT 181 597
Parking	At start		**Ⓓ** NT 179 583
Route terrain	Rough mountain moorland		
Ordnance Survey maps	Landranger 66 (Edinburgh), Explorer 344 (Pentland Hills)		

This fine, fresh, open walk on the eastern slopes of the Pentland Hills ascends Cap Law by way of an ancient and well-defined path, Monks Rig, also known as the Monks Road, to reach the base of the main Pentland ridge below West Kip, to which a short, steep pull is necessary. On the almost parallel descent, there are superb views ahead across the lowlands of the North Esk and South Esk rivers to the distant line of the Moorfoots and Lammermuirs. Route-finding could be difficult in misty conditions.

📝 In the corner of the car park at Nine Mile Burn, go through a gate at a public footpath sign for Balerno by Monks Rig and Braid Law. Go forward along the bottom edge of a hill pasture, and on the far side, turn left now climbing beside a wall.

At the top of the pasture, cross a stile and turn right to another gate, and there go left, climbing once more (signed for Monks Rig), now beside a fence. Keep on as far as a step-stile on the right **Ⓐ**, and over this go across to a wall, beyond which the long steady ascent of Monks Rig awaits. There are grand views ahead across smooth, grassy slopes of the main ridge of the Pentlands.

The path up the hill continues easily, dotted with the bright yellow eyes of tormentil, one of only a few wild flowers that can survive in a windswept

landscape like this, and which manage to do so for quite an extended period during each year.

With no deviation, the grassy route continues towards the dome of Cap Law, with the shapely cone of West Kip peering over its shoulder. Half-way up

A view of the Lammermuir and Moorfoot hills from the Pentlands

Monks Rig is the font stone, presumably so-called because it has become something of a receptacle for small goodwill offerings, but is in reality a cross base that would have served as a wayside marker for the itinerant monks who pioneered this route between valleys.

Approaching Cap Law, the path divides **B**; bear right on a gently descending path that curves round to intercept a clear farm access track below West Kip. The way up West Kip is well trodden, and its summit a fine vantage point, making the ascent well worth the effort. Make the most of the view from the top, which is really quite special, the sort of place where you could sit and meditate quietly on the beauties of the British countryside. Return by the same route to the farm access track.

Back at the track, cross to a stile giving onto a grassy path (signposted for Nine Mile Burn by Braid Law) that curves, descending gently, around the gathering grounds of Eastside Burn, crossing a couple of stiles on the way.

Eventually the accompanying fence line ends. Keep going, and when the track forks near a right of way signpost **C**, bear right to go through a bealach to the north west of Braid Law. Cross the bealach and soon start descending through bracken to cross a burn. The path runs on to cross a stile and wall, beyond which a grassy path, parallel with a fence on the

left, leads across to another stile. Over this, turn left downfield, bearing a little to the right lower down to reach a right of way signpost **D**.

From the signpost, bear right alongside a fence on the left, to join the outward route at a stile and gate at the foot of Monks Rig. Go forward beside a wall for 100 yds, and then cross another stile and go down a field. At the bottom, turn right to return to the starting point. ●

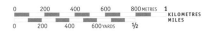

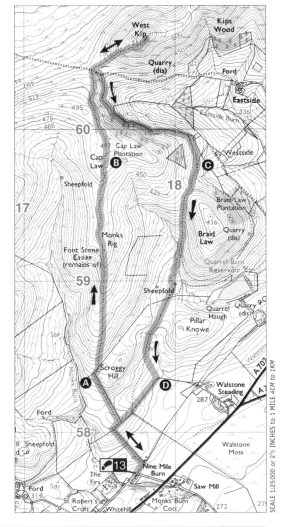

Pencaitland Railway Walk

		GPS waypoints
Start	Crossgatehall	✔ NT 371 689
Finish	Pencaitland	Ⓐ NT 416 697
Distance	5 miles (8.2km)	Ⓑ NT 437 686
Height gain	130 feet (40m)	**FINISH**
Approximate time	2½ hours	NT 454 665
Parking	At start and finish	
Route terrain	Flat railway trackbed through farmland	
Ordnance Survey maps	Landranger 66 (Edinburgh), Explorer 345 (Lammermuir Hills)	

The Pencaitland Railway Walk is a remarkable piece of pathway ingenuity, making the most of an old railway trackbed and linking two particularly attractive villages – Ormiston and Pencaitland. In spite of being linear, and, on the face of it, requiring two cars, the route is served by public transport, but is really such an easy (flat) walk, that you can simply stride out until you have had enough, and then turn round and walk back. Equally, the walk can be done in short sections, and that linking the two villages is especially worthwhile.

Cross head, Colinton

🔲 The walk begins at a small parking area just off the A6124, Musselburgh road.

But before starting it is worth diverting a short distance to visit a virtually unknown monument. A short distance up the nearby B6414, a low gateway in a roadside wall leads to Queen Mary's Monument (NT 374 695). You will have to park awkwardly and then walk through the gate into a narrow neck of woodland to find the monument, which marks the spot where Mary, Queen of Scots surrendered to the Confederate lords on 15 June, 1567. The Scottish nobility, outraged by Mary's marriage to James Hepburn, the fourth Earl of Bothwell, who was widely regarded as a murderer and usurper, rose and defeated a loyalist army at

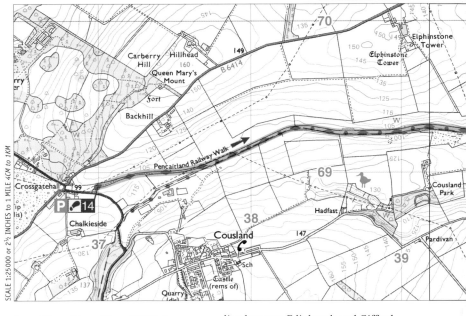

SCALE 1:25000 or 2½ INCHES to 1 MILE 4CM to 1KM

```
0    200   400   600   800 METRES   1
0    200   400   600 YARDS   ½
```
KILOMETRES
MILES

nearby Carberry Hill. On her surrender, Mary was imprisoned in Lochleven Castle, Kinross, where she remained for 11 months.

Throughout the railway walk you encounter a number of 'Memory Stations', small information panels that tell the history of the area, of its people and about what life was like in the days when the railway was operating. The railway between Crossgatehall and Ormiston opened in 1869, and was part of the Edinburgh to Macmerry branch; the line was extended to Gifford in 1901. Coal mining was the main use of this line, but as well as coal it was used for market produce, timber and whisky transportation. The line between Edinburgh and Gifford was hugely popular and carried as many as 30,000 passengers a year.

There is little need for route description; simply follow the railway trackbed, but recognise that it is also appreciated by cyclists.

The route reaches Ormiston at Puddle Bridge **A**, which lies a short way to the north of the village. Ormiston, which has a fine sandstone market (mercat) cross, was the first planned village in

Pencaitland railway walk

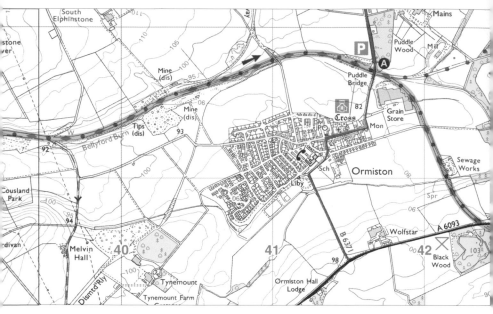

Scotland, founded in 1735 by John Cockburn (1685–1758), one of the initiators of the Agricultural Revolution. The village was the birthplace of the Scottish missionary Robert Moffat (1795–1883), father-in-law of David Livingstone, the missionary and explorer.

Beyond Ormiston, the route continues through endearing countryside that is a delight to wander, as far as the two-part village of Pencaitland, divided by East Lothian's River Tyne into Easter and Wester Pencaitland. The village is virtually unknown outside the locality, but in music circles is renowned for its

Puddle Bridge station

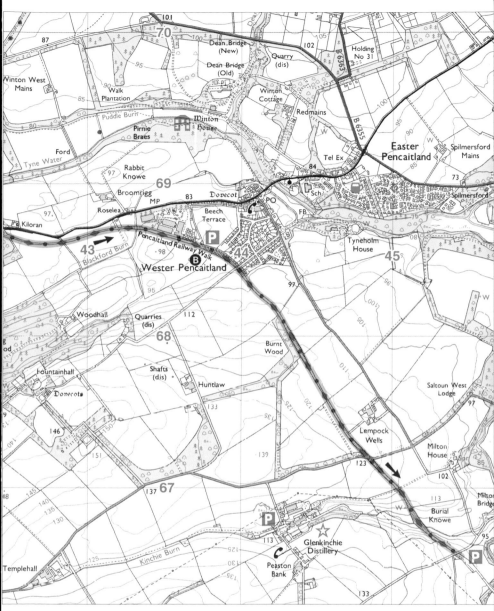

Castlesound Studios, housed in an old primary school, and used over the years by bands such as Runrig, REM and Simple Minds.

The continuing track bypasses Pencaitland, but there is an adjacent car park at the rear of Pencaitland Maltings **B**. From here you can leave the trackbed and take to a stony track leading to the village road, which then lies to the right.

From the maltings, the trackbed route continues a further 1½ miles to conclude, somewhat oddly, opposite a cottage on a side road at Saltoun. There is parking here, and nothing else, but those with two cars at their disposal can effect the complete walk, and then drive to celebrate at the nearby Glenkinchie distillery at Peaston Bank.

Carnethy Hill and Castlelaw Hill Fort

dilapidated wall and a fence. At a corner of both, near a boundary stone, it is possible to use a basic stile to cross the fence.

Press on beyond, walking away from the fence and wall, towards the slopes of Castlelaw Hill, across a short stretch of rough ground, mainly grass and heather until you intercept an obvious broad track running left to right. Turn right on this, descending a little to meet a more pronounced track, which will now form the basis of the next stage of the walk.

Now stride out, enjoying this lovely terraced path and its views of Glencorse Reservoir and the main Pentland Hills. The track improves the farther you go, and eventually runs along the edge of a Military Firing Range (red flags are flown when the range is in use). Continue along the track until you reach a group of buildings **B**, opposite a signpost for a path that descends to Flotterstone. This is the return route, but first, continue along the track, passing

through a nearby gate and then walking towards Castlelaw Farm.

As you approach the farm, a path enters a group of trees, Scots pine and sycamore, to bypass the farm. On the other side, you emerge opposite a car park serving the Castlelaw Hill Fort. Walk across the car park and pass through a gate giving onto a track rising up to the hill fort **C**. This is an Iron Age fort, thought to be more than 2,500 years old, and with an accompanying earth house, or souterrain, built in a nearby ditch and probably used as a grain cellar for the families that lived in the fort. The site is managed by Historic Scotland, and is freely accessible.

Leave the hill fort and walk back to the signpost **B**. There leave the track, and turn left onto a descending path, leading through gorse and by a collapsed wall to reach the road used in the earlier part of the walk. On reaching the road, turn left and retrace your steps to the start. ●

Castlesound Studios, housed in an old primary school, and used over the years by bands such as Runrig, REM and Simple Minds.

The continuing track bypasses Pencaitland, but there is an adjacent car park at the rear of Pencaitland Maltings ⓑ. From here you can leave the trackbed and take to a stony track leading to the village road, which then lies to the right.

From the maltings, the trackbed route continues a further 1½ miles to conclude, somewhat oddly, opposite a cottage on a side road at Saltoun. There is parking here, and nothing else, but those with two cars at their disposal can effect the complete walk, and then drive to celebrate at the nearby Glenkinchie distillery at Peaston Bank. ●

Glencorse Reservoir and Castlelaw Hill Fort

Start	Flotterstone
Distance	5 miles (8km)
Height gain	835 feet (255m)
Approximate time	2½ hours
Parking	At start
Route terrain	Good tracks; country lane; some rough moorland
Ordnance Survey maps	Landranger 66 (Edinburgh), Explorer 344 (Pentland Hills)

GPS waypoints

- NT 233 631
- Ⓐ NT 215 640
- Ⓑ NT 216 636
- Ⓒ NT 229 639

Glencorse is beautiful enough, but when viewed from the slopes of Castlelaw Hill, backed by the curvaceous profiles of the main Pentland ridge, the reservoir and its surroundings take on an altogether more pleasing aspect. For once there is a harmonious relationship between the efforts of man and those of Nature, each complimenting the other, and bringing a satisfying synergy to the scene.

Between the shores of the reservoir and the slopes of Castlelaw Hill lies a little rugged crossing, nothing unduly difficult, but with a brief, steep descent, followed by a brief, steep ascent. This should deter no one, but there is a shortcut if anyone feels disinclined to take it on.

Leave the car park at the Flotterstone Visitor Centre, and walk along a pathway through a narrow belt of trees, parallel with the road. Eventually, the path emerges onto the road. Just before it does, you pass a blue plaque commemorating Charles Thomson Rees Wilson (1869–1959), who was born at nearby Cross House Farm in Glencorse parish, the son of a farmer, and who went on to become Noble Laureate in Physics as the inventor of the 'Cloud Chamber', a device used for detecting particles of ionizing radiation.

Continue along the road, with ever-improving views of the reservoir and its backdrop of hills; small clusters of rocks and branches at the water's edge provide a resting place for cormorants.

Just after passing a small plantation on the right, at NT 219 639, you reach the foot of a path (signposted for Castlelaw) running upwards along the plantation boundary. This leads up to the path used on the return leg, and might be used as a shortcut for anyone uncertain about the interlude of rough ground that lies ahead. At the top, you turn right.

Press on alongside the reservoir until both road and reservoir abruptly change direction. A few strides beyond the

bend, leave the road by passing through a gate **A** on the right, beyond which lies a rough stony track leading to Colinton and Balerno. Almost immediately abandon the stony track in favour of a broad grassy path rising gently on the right onto a low hill.

As you climb, the track gradually swings to the right, towards the steep-sided ravine of Kirk Burn, which has to be crossed. So, when you first reach a spread of bracken, leave the path and bear right, descending steeply and with care into the ravine. Cross the burn, which in places is narrow enough to step over, and then climb equally steeply on the other side to reach a

Glencorse Reservoir

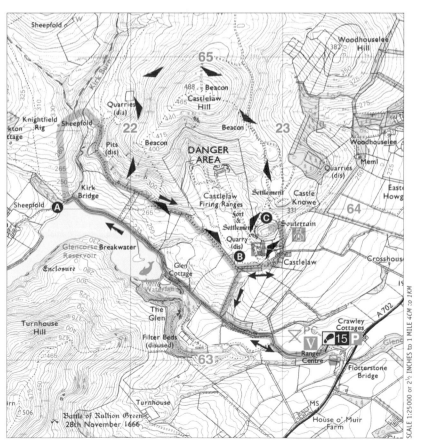

SCALE 1:25000 or 2½ INCHES to 1 MILE 4CM to 1KM

Carnethy Hill and Castlelaw Hill Fort

dilapidated wall and a fence. At a corner of both, near a boundary stone, it is possible to use a basic stile to cross the fence.

Press on beyond, walking away from the fence and wall, towards the slopes of Castlelaw Hill, across a short stretch of rough ground, mainly grass and heather until you intercept an obvious broad track running left to right. Turn right on this, descending a little to meet a more pronounced track, which will now form the basis of the next stage of the walk.

Now stride out, enjoying this lovely terraced path and its views of Glencorse Reservoir and the main Pentland Hills. The track improves the farther you go, and eventually runs along the edge of a Military Firing Range (red flags are flown when the range is in use). Continue along the track until you reach a group of buildings **B**, opposite a signpost for a path that descends to Flotterstone. This is the return route, but first, continue along the track, passing

through a nearby gate and then walking towards Castlelaw Farm.

As you approach the farm, a path enters a group of trees, Scots pine and sycamore, to bypass the farm. On the other side, you emerge opposite a car park serving the Castlelaw Hill Fort. Walk across the car park and pass through a gate giving onto a track rising up to the hill fort **C**. This is an Iron Age fort, thought to be more than 2,500 years old, and with an accompanying earth house, or souterrain, built in a nearby ditch and probably used as a grain cellar for the families that lived in the fort. The site is managed by Historic Scotland, and is freely accessible.

Leave the hill fort and walk back to the signpost **B**. There leave the track, and turn left onto a descending path, leading through gorse and by a collapsed wall to reach the road used in the earlier part of the walk. On reaching the road, turn left and retrace your steps to the start.   ●

Braid Hills

Start	Blackford		

Start	Blackford
Distance	5 miles (8km)
Height gain	1,000 feet (305m)
Approximate time	2½ hours
Parking	Blackford Pond
Route terrain	Woodland trails; burnside paths; golf course; open hilltop; some road walking
Ordnance Survey maps	Landranger 66 (Edinburgh), Explorer 350 (Edinburgh)

GPS waypoints

- 🗺 NT 255 709
- Ⓐ NT 257 703
- Ⓑ NT 257 693
- Ⓒ NT 244 695
- Ⓓ NT 240 695
- Ⓔ NT 244 702
- Ⓕ NT 256 703

This lovely walk is very close to the centre of Edinburgh, and the whole area of the Braid Hills is quite an agreeable surprise, a splendid place to amble, full of interest and with stunning, far-reaching views. This walk does not ascend Blackford Hill, but that can easily be included by a clear and obvious route.

🗺 Set off from the small car park at Blackford Pond by turning right onto a broad track that soon passes the pond with its resident population of birdlife. The path passes allotment gardens and continues around Blackford Hill, passing along the edge of woodland, a habitat favoured by red campion, foxglove, elder, gorse and invasive Indian balsam. Soon, the path merges with another below Blackford Hill. Keep right, soon descending through stands of sycamore, beech, elder and hawthorn.

When the path divides, branch right, continuing to descend, now more steeply to reach a kissing-gate. Through this, keep left to join a level track bearing left Ⓐ, alongside Braid Burn and passing old quarries on the left.

Carry on to reach Howe Dean Path on the right, at a Nature Reserve information panel. Here, turn right, crossing a footbridge and going up

Howe Dean Path as it climbs beside a burn through a wooded gorge. Established sycamore and understorey fill this delightful ravine through which the path climbs steadily, crossing the burn and continuing to fenced steps leading up to a higher path.

Stay on the path to a kissing-gate at the upper boundary of the nature

Meadow vetch

reserve. Cross a road (Braid Hills Drive), and go on to a golf course opposite. A broad track strikes out onto the golf course, and, because the route crosses a number of fairways, it would be wise to keep your eyes open and move quickly.

When the track forks, bear left, the track now climbing a little. As the rising track turns left and abruptly ends, go forward, maintaining the original direction along a path flanked by gorse bushes. At the top of the path, keep heading the same way, now along a broad green sward, crossing more fairways finally to reach a red shale path .

Turn right along the shale path, soon walking alongside a wall. Here is a good place to keep an eye open for bullfinches, immaculately dapper little birds, the male boasting a deep red chest, black cap and a conspicuous white rump. Follow the shale path, leaving it momentarily to climb to the top of a low hill topped by a trig pillar and topograph.

The view from the top of Braid Hills embraces notably the Seven Hills of Edinburgh: Arthur's Seat, Blackford Hill, Braid Hills, Calton Hill, Castle Rock, Corstophine Hill and Craiglockhart Hill. But the extent of the panorama almost defies belief, reaching to Ben Lomond, 58 miles away, Ben Vorlich, 65 miles, Ben More and Stob Binnein, 61 miles and 60 miles respectively.

Continue across the top of the hill to rejoin the shale path, which soon starts to descend. When the path forks, branch left and walk down to meet a road **C**. *Take care as you emerge onto the road: there is no roadside footpath and the exit is close to a blind summit.* Cross the road and turn right. Take the first turning on the left (Riselaw Crescent), and follow this round to meet an A-road (Pentland Terrace/Comiston Road). Cross and turn right, walking beside a fence for about 100 yds, and then turn left into Braidburn Valley Park, bearing left to walk through an avenue of trees.

When the path merges with another, bear right and descend to meet Braid Burn once more **D**. Keep right, above the burn, crossing it at the second footbridge and turning right along a surfaced pathway. Keep an eye open here for clusters of monkey flower and

Blackford Pond

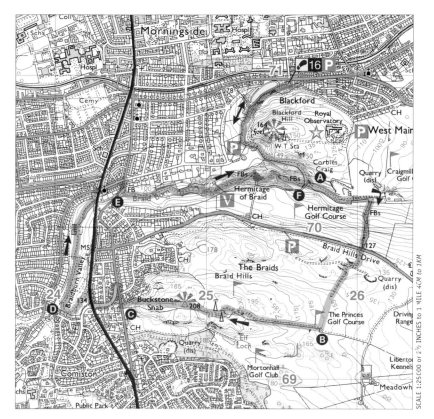

SCALE 1:25C00 or 2½ INCHES to 1 MILE 4CM to 1KM

0	200	400	600	800 METRES	1	
					KILOMETRES	
					MILES	
0	200	400	600 YARDS	½		

forget-me-not alongside the burn and the long strand-like stems and delicate white flowers of river-water crowfoot, which actually flourish in the water.

Shortly after the burn enters a culvert, walk up to park gates and turn right to a major road junction. Go into the road opposite, passing Greenbank parish church. Continue for about 200 yds to another junction at a roundabout, and here turn right into Braid Road. A few strides farther on, go left into the Hermitage of Braid Nature Reserve **E**.

The Hermitage of Braid and its grounds were gifted to the City of Edinburgh by John McDougal, and officially opened by the then Lord Provost in June 1938. The area is believed to have been named after a former Sheriff of Edinburgh, Henri de Brad, who was a major landowner here during the 12th century.

Cross a bridge spanning Braid Burn, and keep forward on a surfaced driveway that leads to the Hermitage, now housing the visitor centre. Continue past the centre, always following the burnside path, which changes banks a few times before finally passing beneath a wooden footbridge **G**.

Just after the footbridge, leave the track and bear left up steps to a kissing-gate where the outward route is joined. Beyond the gate climb steadily on a stony track that soon levels as it passes through woodland. When the track forks, bear left, descending gently and going back past Blackford Pond to complete the walk. ●

Allermuir Hill and Capelaw Hill

		GPS waypoints
Start	Swanston	
Distance	5 miles (8km)	✐ NT 240 674
Height gain	1,295 feet (395m)	Ⓐ NT 236 666
		Ⓑ NT 217 663
Approximate time	3 hours	Ⓒ NT 217 666
		Ⓓ NT 222 671
Parking	Swanston (use the designated Pentland Hills Regional Park car park, just past the golf club)	
Route terrain	Grassy mountain slopes with good paths throughout	
Ordnance Survey maps	Landranger 66 (Edinburgh), Explorer 344 (Pentland Hills)	

It is usual to combine the ascent of Allermuir Hill with nearby Caerketton Hill, but here the route looks farther west, and runs out to embrace the grassy summit of Capelaw Hill, from where it slips northwards towards Dreghorn, before striking across country along the northern base of the Pentland Hills, back to the starting point. The view throughout is stunning, not only to the north of the city of Edinburgh and across the Firth of Forth to Fife, but also to the south, to the neat, moulded groups of hills that comprise this exquisite regional park.

The walk begins from the small village of Swanston, which grew up in the early 18th century around a farm, and originally consisted of ten thatched cottages. The cottages remain, but renovation work in the 1960s saw the outer walls being retained but the ten cottages made into seven.

Swanston Cottage was built in 1761, and was leased by the parents of Robert Louis Stevenson, Thomas and Margaret (neé Balfour) between 1867 and 1880. Robert Louis Stevenson spent several summers here, and set his novel *St Ives* in the village.

✐ Cross the car park and take to a path climbing through a compact stand

of trees to emerge at Swanston village. Keep on to pass white-washed cottages, and go through a kissing-gate, after which you take to a rising path along the edge of the golf course. As the path descends briefly to cross a burn, continue climbing on the other side, beside a fence. Ignore the first gap on the left, and continue instead to a field gate and kissing-gate (marked 'Sheep enclosure').

Through the gate, continue ascending amid low-lying gorse, and with a fine retrospective view over Edinburgh. A short way farther on, when the track divides, branch left and, continuing to climb through gorse, to intercept a grassy track just below the remains of a wall. Here, turn left and soon arrive at a signpost **Ⓐ**. Leave the main track at this point, and branch right for Allermuir, climbing steeply on a grassy path to a shallow col just to the south of Mullieputchie.

Press on along a clear grassy path, bearing right when it forks a short way farther on. Continue to aptly named Windy Door Nick, beyond which a short pull takes you up beside a fence onto Allermuir Hill, topped by a trig pillar and a viewpoint indicator etched with a huge amount of landscape information.

Go through the gate on the summit and walk down beside a fence to a corner (boundary stone nearby), and then continue descending with the fence. Just a short way down the slope, however, branch right towards Capelaw Hill, crossing a broad track lower down

before reaching a gate and ladder-stile.

Take the broad grassy track up onto Capelaw Hill, one of the few points to give a distinctive image of Allermuir Hill. The summit is marked by a large, metal double-pole. At the summit, turn right (north) onto a path heading towards Edinburgh. Much lower down when you intercept a broad track **Ⓑ**, turn left and follow it round the low hill in front of you (although you can just as easily go over the hill). The track leads down to a gate at a fence junction **Ⓒ**. Continue, descending gently on a grassy track, passing a blue-banded waymark pole, where the track swings to the right. Follow this down through stands of gorse, keeping an eye open for a solitary building at the foot of

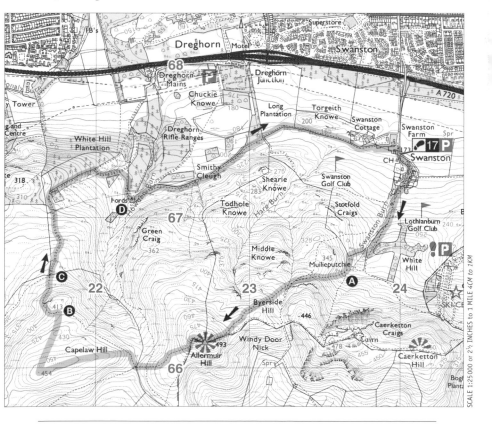

On the summit of Allermuir Hill

Howden Burn, off to the right. The path you are walking gently swings that way and drops to intercept another broad track. Turn right to the building **ⓓ**, where there is a signpost.

Turn left onto the track for Dreghorn, but when you reach a gate at NT 224 672, branch right onto a path that passes around the edge of a small plantation. The going is a little muddy in places, but this is short-lived, and beyond the end of the plantation you maintain the same direction along a

narrow path that later joins a broader path, leading down to a fence along the boundary of three successive small stands of trees.

After the final plantation you pass through a gate onto a broad vehicular track, and press on along the edge of a golf course, all the way back to Swanston. As you reach Swanston Farm turn immediately right through a gate onto the edge of the golf course, but then turn left to walk to and across the golf course car park to reach the village road. Turn right to complete the walk. ●

Bonaly Country Park and Harbour Hill

		GPS waypoints
Start	Bonaly Country Park	✒ NT 212 676
Distance	5½ miles (9km)	Ⓐ NT 210 671
Height gain	1,015 feet (310m)	Ⓑ NT 187 668
Approximate time	3 hours	Ⓒ NT 204 649
Parking	At start	Ⓓ NT 210 657
Route terrain	Reservoir trails; rough tracks; open moorland; woodland	
Ordnance Survey maps	Landranger 66 (Edinburgh), Explorer 344 (Pentland Hills)	

This excellent circuit contrasts the delights of reservoir tracks with open mountain moorland at the very northern edge of the Pentland Hills. The Bonaly Country Park has long been a place of popular resort, and the extension to visit the reservoirs and effect an ancient cross-glen passage, one that has been pursued by the people of Edinburgh and its suburbs for generations. The ascent of Harbour Hill can be avoided by the simple expedient of passing it to the south, but this does add rather more to the walk; crossing the hill, while briefly steep, is mainly on grass and heather, and succumbs easily to a steady plod.

✒ Pass through the gate at the end of the car park, and walk ahead on a broad stony track for Glencorse, which rises steadily into a Scots pine and larch plantation. Just before leaving the plantation at its top edge, turn right Ⓐ along a path through the trees and parallel with the top boundary fence *(beware slippery tree roots)*. This leads to a gate from which a constructed path leads on through gates and down to a broad track that links the Torduff and Clubbiedean Reservoirs.

Turn left along the track (signed for East Kinleith), and walk on to cross below the dam of Clubbiedean, after which the track swings left and accompanies the reservoir to its far end. There a left and right keep you on the track, which now leads to Middle and Easter Kinleith farms. Here, turn left along a surfaced lane and walk as far as a turning on the left Ⓑ at a road junction.

The rough road that now runs roughly in a southerly direction is superb walking and has long been known as Ranges Road; it leads up to be joined by another from the Ranger Centre near Harlaw Farm. Once united, continue to follow the clear track as it climbs the slopes of Harbour Hill to the col (bealach) Ⓒ between Harbour Hill and Bell's Hill at the head of Maiden Cleuch.

Turn left here beside a fence and plod up the slopes of Harbour Hill, nothing like so demanding as might be expected.

If you want to avoid this ascent, then the alternative is to continue across the col and down into Maiden Cleuch until *you reach a signpost from which a track branches left around Harbour Hill, signed for Bonaly. This variant will increase the distance to 7 miles (11km)*

Harbour Hill

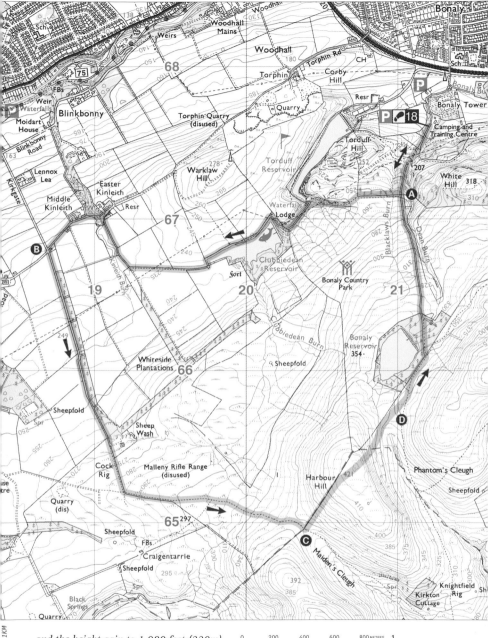

and the height gain to 1,080 feet (330m), and a good broad path leads the way.

If sticking to the original line, then from the summit of Harbour Hill simply descend in a north-easterly direction on grass through heather aiming for the broad bealach **D** between Harbour Hill and Capelaw Hill. Now this good path slips down past Bonaly Reservoir and back across open moorland to the plantation boundary **A**, reaching it at a gate, through which you simply retrace your steps to the Bonaly car park. ●

Monynut Edge

		GPS waypoints
Start	Upper Monynut Forest, where road descends to Monynut Water	

Start	Upper Monynut Forest, where road descends to Monynut Water
Distance	5½ miles (8.8km)
Height gain	1,065 feet (325m)
Approximate time	3 hours
Parking	At start
Route terrain	Forest trails; open moorland
Ordnance Survey maps	Landranger 67 (Duns, Dunbar & Eyemouth), Explorer 345 (Lammermuir Hills)

GPS waypoints

- ✔ NT 694 676
- Ⓐ NT 699 663
- Ⓑ NT 710 653
- Ⓒ NT 712 654
- Ⓓ NT 715 666
- Ⓔ NT 695 686

Monynut Edge is a lonely corner of the northern Lammermuirs with its western slopes largely covered by forest. A good track goes through the forest and gives enjoyable walking. After leaving the forest the route climbs rough ground to join a track to Packman's Grave and then descends to the road. The varied terrain and the isolation of these beautiful hills make this a memorable walk, but the return leg should only be undertaken in clear conditions. The possibility of wading through a burn suggests that carrying a small towel and a change of socks in your day sack is a good idea.

The walk starts from the point where the road going eastwards through the forest crosses Monynut Water. Take the forest track, which climbs the side of the hill to the east of the burn, ascending gently south-eastwards. It begins to descend when it reaches a point opposite a white house on the other side of the valley (Upper Monynut). Cross the burn Ⓐ and climb again. There are excellent views of Monynut Edge and Heart Law, which the walker will climb later.

When the track swings sharply to the right Ⓑ at a hairpin bend, leave it by turning left down a heathery firebreak through which there is a distinct path. Near the bottom this passes through dense and prickly pine trees. Persevere

to reach the stream and cross it close to a fence Ⓒ – you may have to take boots off and wade across if the burn is in spate.

Now head northwards to climb Camy Cleugh Rig, crossing the burn and taking the clearest path. This will be hard work, but soon Short Crib Burn, a formidable gully, comes into view on the left. The track going to Packman's Grave runs close to the top of the gully and one of the meandering sheep tracks will take you to it as you keep heading northwards Ⓓ.

The track maintains the northerly direction, with fine views down to the forest to the left. This is an exhilarating ridge walk, but the track becomes less distinct when it meets a fence below

Wester Dod. The triangulation pillar on the summit 1,352 feet (412m) may be clearly seen through a gateway. After the next gate the track degenerates further. Continue to walk by a fence. There is a radio mast to the right, and just to the left of this the cement works on the coast near Dunbar can be clearly seen.

There is no sign of Packman's Grave at the point where the track meets two fences **E**. Although nothing survives to tell us who the peddler was or how he died the map bestows an aura of sadness to the spot.

From the site of the grave descend close to the forest to the road and turn left. A few minutes of pleasant walking brings you back to the road bridge across Monynut Water. ●

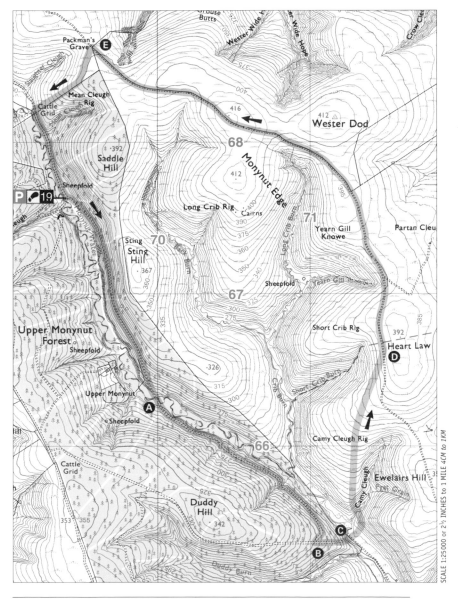

SCALE 1:25000 or 2½ INCHES to 1 MILE 4CM to 1KM

River Almond Walk

		GPS waypoints
Start	East Calder	
Distance	5¾ miles (9.2km)	✔ NT 092 682
Height gain	575 feet (175m)	Ⓐ NT 088 688
		Ⓑ NT 092 693
Approximate time	3 hours	Ⓒ NT 098 696
Parking	Car park at East Calder entrance to country park	Ⓓ NT 106 706
		Ⓔ NT 101 709
		Ⓕ NT 086 685
Route terrain	Woodland trails; riverside paths	
Ordnance Survey maps	Landranger 65 (Falkirk & Linlithgow), Explorer 350 (Edinburgh)	

Tucked away in the valley of the River Almond, the country park on which this walk is based is full of interest and has a fascinating history. The walk is based on two adjoining estates – Almondell and Calderwood – and can be a surprisingly time-consuming place to explore in spite of its modest size.

✔ Begin from the car park on the edge of East Calder by walking back towards the entrance, but soon turning right onto a woodland footpath that emerges at an information panel adjoining a surfaced estate road. Turn right and follow the road, flanked by hazel, ash, hawthorn, elder, wild cherry, copper beech and sycamore, as far as the crenulated Almondell Bridge Ⓐ.

Alexander Naysmith who was also a talented landscape artist and believed to have painted the only authentic portrait of Robert Burns built the bridge in 1800. A small bridge crosses a burn and an old stone records that it was built in 1784 by Margaret, Countess of Buchan. This part of the walk is especially glorious in autumn.

Immediately before the bridge, turn right onto an ascending woodland path that leads through delightful mixed woodland to meet a higher path along the top edge. Turn left along this path, which runs on along a woodland

boundary, and then turns back into the body of the woodland, going down a long flight of steps to emerge at a path not far from a suspension bridge built in 1970 by the Royal Engineers Ⓑ.

Beyond the suspension bridge climb to a path that strikes westwards above the riverbank (do not climb the steps). Climb over a stile and walk with the feeder stream to the right. Cross a lane and follow the signs to Lin's Mill Aqueduct. Many more stiles are crossed, but the path is grassy and there are wide views. Eventually the path enters a wood and then divides as it passes beneath electric lines Ⓒ. Go left here and cross the canal feeder in a meadow where it emerges through a brick portal and then take the path along its left-hand bank.

The route is now straightforward as it follows the feeder stream, which occasionally vanishes underground for short sections. There are glimpses of the river far below – the grand house

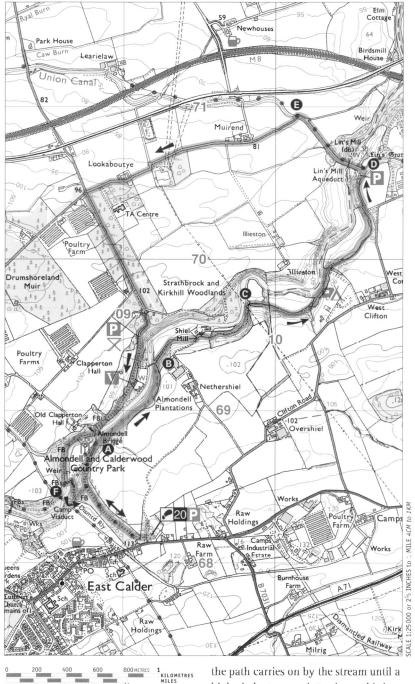

SCALE 1:25000 or 2½ INCHES to 1 MILE 4CM to 1KM

0	200	400	600	800 METRES	1
					KILOMETRES
					MILES
0	200	400	600 YARDS	½	

opposite is Illieston, originally a royal hunting lodge but remodelled as a residence in 1665. After crossing a track the path carries on by the stream until a high viaduct comes into view – this is the aqueduct, which takes the Union Canal across the Almond Valley. Soon afterwards you climb steps to a lane. Turn left and keep left when the lane divides to pass beneath the aqueduct **D**. There used to be a mill on the river at this point owned by William Lin, who in 1645 was the last man to die of plague in Scotland.

Go up the steps to the right of the green gate to the north towpath and cross the aqueduct. In 1895 an enormous icicle grew from an arch of the viaduct to reach the surface of the river 120 feet (36m) below. Certainly the height is spectacular and may not be to everyone's taste. When the towpath reaches the other side there is a section where its original granite setts are still to be seen.

Cross the canal at the first bridge **E** and walk down a track to join a road at Muirend. Pass a property named Lookaboutye and, on the left, a drive to Drumshoreland House and turn left at crossroads on to the driveway into the Country Park. This takes you directly to the Visitor Centre, which stands on the site of Almondell House, built c1790 by Henry Erskine, brother of the 11th earl of Buchan. He designed it himself but proved to be a poor architect – the roof leaked, foundations became waterlogged, and timber shrank because it was not properly seasoned. He even built the icehouse facing south! Consequently the mansion became dangerously dilapidated, finally being pulled down in 1969.

Follow the drive past the Visitor Centre (the astronomical pillar in front is from another Erskine home nearby, Kirkhill House at Broxburn) following the surfaced road until it returns to

Almondell Bridge, East Calder

Almondell Bridge **A**. Do not cross the bridge, but go to the right of it on a descending track that runs along the wooded banks of the River Almond.

When the red waymarked route bears left, turn with it, walking across a footbridge with an aqueduct suspended beneath it **F**. Built in 1820 at the time of the construction of the Union Canal, the aqueduct takes the form of a trough on a cantilevered support slung beneath the footbridge; it carries the canal feeder stream over the River Almond.

On the other side of the river, turn right, climbing steps onto a path high above the river. When the path forks, branch left, and shortly left again through woodland to rejoin the main surfaced driveway. Turn right and walk back to the information panel, and there keep left through woodland to return to the car park. ●

Priestlaw Hill

		GPS waypoints
Start	Whiteadder Reservoir	
Distance	6½ miles (10.5km)	✎ NT 646 642
Height gain	1,000 feet (305m)	Ⓐ NT 644 637
		Ⓑ NT 635 612
Approximate time	3½ hours	Ⓒ NT 651 609
Parking	Small car park to the east of the bridge at the western end of the reservoir, on the B6355	Ⓓ NT 652 630
Route terrain	Farm tracks and mountain moorland	
Ordnance Survey maps	Landranger 67 (Duns, Dunbar & Eyemouth), Explorer 345 (Lammermuir Hills)	

The outward part of the route is easy walking on a track, grassy at times, following Faseny Water as it courses down through the hills. This burn is one of the scenic delights of a walk into lonely countryside where it will be a surprise to meet other walkers. The return begins on a clearly marked path, but the descent from the summit of Priestlaw Hill is over rough heather and care is needed both in protecting ankles as well as in navigation.

✎ Turn out of the parking space and cross the bridge spanning the northern arm of the reservoir, then take the lane which heads south past the top of the reservoir, signposted to Priestlaw Farm. Turn right Ⓐ before the bridge towards Penshiel.

Just before a white bungalow, turn right through a gate onto a hill track that climbs steadily away from the reservoir. In a field to the left of the track are the scant remains of a grange, probably belonging to Abbey St Bathans to the east, while to the right is a chapel stone, a reminder of religious persecution in former times when Catholics were forced to worship in remote locations. The track is level and grassy for a while and you will often encounter curlew, skylark and grouse as well as innumerable rabbits.

The track soon becomes stony again,

Whiteadder Reservoir

although the walking is most enjoyable with Faseny Water below to the left. There are some delightful picnic sites on its banks. Continue walking southwards and turn left when you reach the road **B**.

The road climbs steeply and serves as a county boundary for part of this stretch. After about one mile, and just after the summit of the climb, there is a gate on the left **C**. Go through this and bear left when the track divides to follow a rough track marked with wooden posts, which climbs the western flank of Priestlaw Hill. The track leads to a point below the extensive summit cairn. Climb up to this and then continue north to a smaller cairn, which

Kell Burn feeds the Whiteadder Reservoir

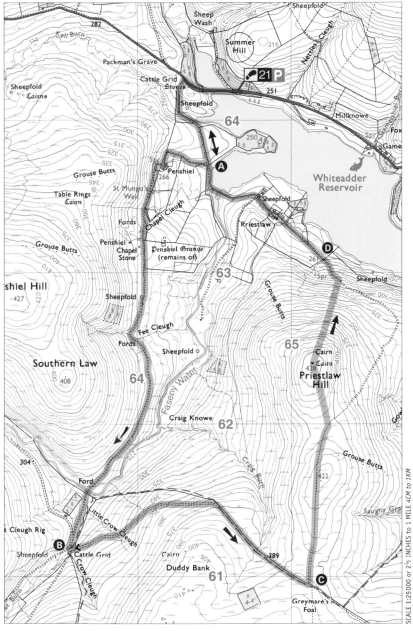

SCALE 1:25000 or 2½ INCHES to 1 MILE 4CM to 1KM

0	200	400	600	800 METRES	1
					KILOMETRES
					MILES
0	200	400	600 YARDS	½	

provides an even better view.

Descend from the hill roughly in a northerly direction, down heather-covered slopes. Aim to the right of Priestlaw Farm where a gate  leads into the pastures – take care over the rough ground. Then, having passed through the gate, walk down a farm track and go through the farmyard. Cross the reservoir bridge, and go forward to rejoin your outward route, and then retrace your steps to the starting point.

●

John Muir Way

Start	Cockenzie	
Finish	Aberlady	
Distance	7½ miles (12km)	
Height gain	165 feet (50m)	
Approximate time	3½ hours	
Parking	At start and finish	
Route terrain	Easy footpaths; sandy shoreline	
Ordnance Survey maps	Landranger 66 (Edinburgh), Explorer 351 (Dunbar & North Berwick)	

GPS waypoints

- ✍ NT 391 750
- Ⓐ NT 416 759
- Ⓑ NT 442 777
- Ⓒ NT 449 789
- Ⓓ NT 462 801
- **FINISH**
- NT 465 799

It is appropriate that part of the impressive stretch of coastline between Prestonpans and Dunbar, an area of low cliffs, off-shore skerries, dunes and saltmarsh, should have been created a country park named after John Muir, and that a fine trail along the coast constructed in his honour, for this native of Dunbar was one of the pioneers of the National Park movement in the USA. The walk necessarily is linear, but is well served with public transport, making it easy enough to park at one end and take a bus back to the start. Although often sandwiched between the road and the shore, all your attention is focused seaward, and there are many places where you can simply walk off the Way onto the sand.

✍ At the start there is a large parking area (signed from the B1348), just to the south-west of a power station; on the face of it, an

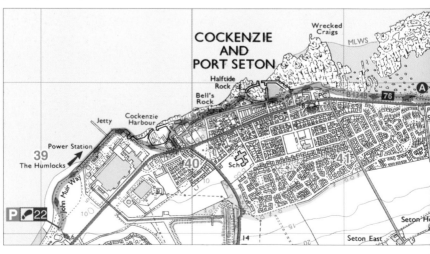

inauspicious place to begin, but from the car park, a surfaced path speeds you round the power station to Cockenzie and Port Seton Pier, and then through an elongated residential area before emerging on the road.

Very soon, all this urbanism is left behind and you find yourself at the edge of Seton Sands **Ⓐ**, a popular holiday destination, and able to spend more time walking through dunes, rocky interludes and coastal strands. Although traffic is never far away, the shoreline is such that you can wander freely, and spend time birdwatching as you go. The whole stretch of coastline is popular with birdlife, and it is not unusual to see shelduck, red-breasted mergansers, redshank, curlew, lapwing, oystercatcher, pink-footed geese, wigeon and flocks of golden plover, especially in autumn and through the winter months.

As you round the rocky headland of Ferny Ness so you move on to reach Gosford Bay **Ⓑ**, which holds a vast range of wildfowl, wader, gull, tern, skua and many sea birds. The bay lies to the north of Gosford Estate whose

ornate sandstone gate pillars and gate lodges are passed en route, across the road, and whose mansion, Gosford House, the family seat of the Charteris family, was built in the 1790s to a design by Robert Adam for the sixth Earl of Wemyss. The house and estate is open to the public during summer months.

As you wander along Gosford Sands, the John Muir Way keeps close to the road in readiness for what is known as the Aberlady Mile. Approaching an area of scrub, the path crosses a narrow bridge **Ⓒ**, and then presses on past anti-tank blocks built during the Second World War, to reach the lush green woodland of Green Craig. The

MAP CONTINUES ON NEXT PAGE →

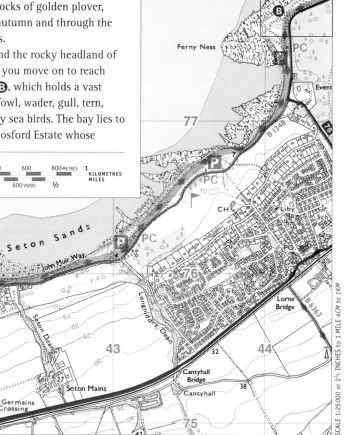

SCALE 1:25000 or 2½ INCHES to 1 MILE 4CM to 1KM

path stays within the grounds of Green Craig, and then continues to Aberlady, separated from the road by a low wall until virtually the last moment. This is the most direct route. However, once across that narrow bridge **C**, you can turn left at the edge of scrub for a few strides to reach the beach – or take to the sandy coast a little sooner.

Now simply walk along the beach until, beyond Green Craig, you can follow a shoreline path, later surfaced as it serves Craigielaw golf course. The path passes Craigielaw Point and then moves on to Aberlady Point before joining the golf course access. Follow this, but keep an eye open for a sign-posted path to the remains of Kilspindie

Castle **D**, due north of the church.

All that remains of 16th-century Kilspindie Castle is the base of a doorway with a length of wall that comes to an oval gun loop, built for the powerful Douglas family. Locally the Douglas family held several towers, including Whittinghame, Longniddry and eventually Kilspindie.

Beyond Kilspindie Castle, you can complete a little circular walk through the field in which the castle remains are found, or walk back to the surfaced golf course access. Turn right, and you soon reach the centre of Aberlady, or turn left for a short distance to a narrow, enclosed path that leads around the churchyard to the main road. ●

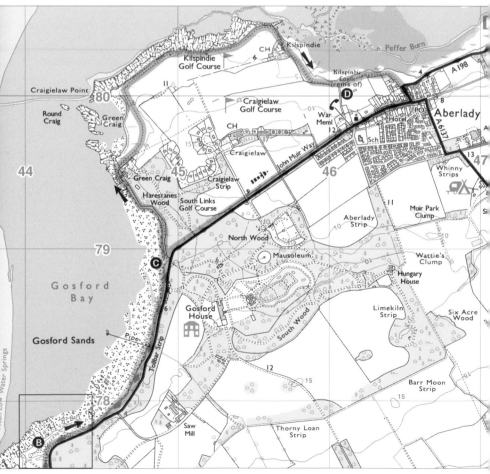

Pentland Ridge and Logan Burn

		GPS waypoints	
Start	Flotterstone		NT 233 631
Distance	6¾ miles (11km)	**Ⓐ**	NT 229 631
Height gain	1,755 feet (535m)	**Ⓑ**	NT 208 623
Approximate time	4 hours	**Ⓒ**	NT 195 615
Parking	At start	**Ⓓ**	NT 185 609
Route terrain	Mountain upland, mainly grass; road walking	**Ⓔ**	NT 189 621
Ordnance Survey maps	Landranger 66 (Edinburgh), Explorer 344 (Pentland Hills)		

The outward section of this delectable Pentland ridge walk is demanding, entailing a steep ascent and then a switchback ridge walk. *The way back is a level walk by the shores of the two reservoirs with fine views of the hills traversed earlier.* There are few distinguishing features along the ridge, suggesting that it should not be attempted if visibility is poor. *Scald Law (1,898 feet/579m), the highest summit of the Pentlands, features in Walk 24, but strong walkers may wish to embrace it within the present walk. This extension is given at the end of the route description.*

Turn right from the car park to head towards Glencorse Reservoir and join a footpath passing the visitor centre that winds through trees by the side of the road. The path passes a plaque dedicated to C T R Wilson who was born nearby at Crosshouse Farm in 1869. Information about Wilson is given in Walk 15.

Soon the path merges with the road and about 50 yds farther on a path leaves on the left waymarked to Scald Law **Ⓐ**. Take this, cross the bridge and bear right following a Pentland Way waymark. The broad grassy track is the start of a lengthy and undulating climb over Turnhouse Hill and Carnethy Hill.

Below Turnhouse Hill is the site of the Battle of Rullion Green, fought on November 28, 1666 between a force of Covenanters retreating from a march on Edinburgh and the men of General Thomas Dalziel (Tam Dalyell), who overtook them and slaughtered them for the 'defence of the covenanting work of the Reformation'. Turnhouse Hill itself provides a spectacular view through 360°, although Glencorse Reservoir is completely hidden. This is a lovely spot, and worth visiting while you take a breather.

Descend White Craig Heads to the wall **Ⓑ** before beginning another pull to the top of Carnethy Hill. The stone-strewn summit, the site of a Bronze Age

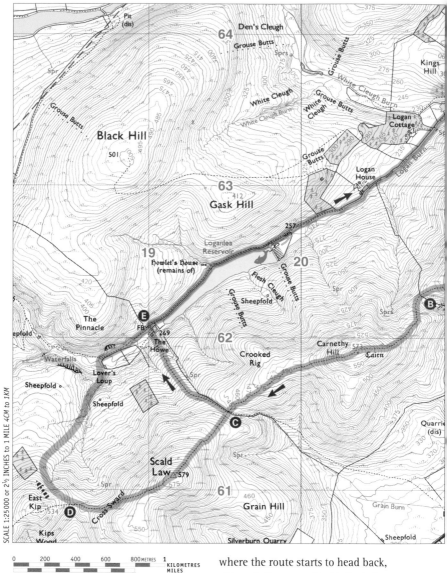

```
0    200    400    600    800 METRES  1
                                         KILOMETRES
                                         MILES
0    200    400    600 YARDS  ½
```

cairn, gives a good view of Glencorse Reservoir, but now Loganlea is hidden.

Continue on the ridge path by dropping down to the col (bealach) **C**, where a path from Penicuik, a long-established and much-used link with Balerno, joins from the south east. Edinburgh and the Firth of Forth can be seen to the north through a gap in the hills. This ancient pass is the place where the route starts to head back, although those wanting to include Scald Law do so from here.

Otherwise, turn right off the ridge path on to the Kirk Road, descend directly to the head of Loganlea Reservoir **E**, and then turn right along the road and beside Logan Burn to complete the return to Flotterstone.

Extension to Scald Law
Overall distance: 8 miles (13km)
Overall height gain: 2,180 feet (665m)

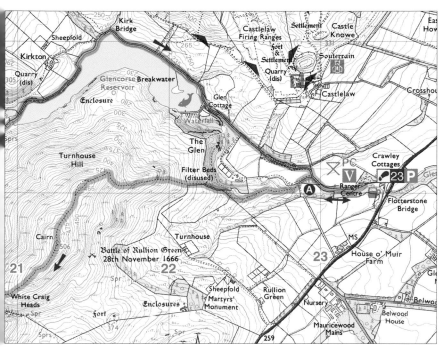

From the col **C** engage a brisk climb
to the top of Scald Law at 1,898 feet
(579m) the highest of the Pentland
summits. On reaching the top, pause to
study the terrain from here and note
particularly the plantation to the west
and the gully lower down (Lover's
Loup). The descending route is on the
west side of the gully and a path can
be clearly seen leaving the ridge
northwards towards the wood.

When the ridge path divides, fork
right and descend to another col **D**, and
there turn right
again on a clear
path heading
north. Go through
a gate and
continue to
descend with a
fence to the right.
A perfect view of
both Glencorse
and Loganlea
reservoirs now
comes into view

as height is lost with a farmhouse in
the foreground to give scale to the vista.
Turn right at the bottom to join the right
of way and follow this to the road
serving the reservoirs where the main
route joins **E**.

At weekends the road may be busy
with cyclists and anglers' cars. The walk
back to the car park is enjoyable for its
views of the hills you have walked
earlier in the day. ●

The Pentland Hills from near Flotterstone

Scald Hill and two Kips

Start	Threipmuir Reservoir	
Distance	7½ miles (12km)	
Height gain	1,885 feet (575m)	
Approximate time	4 hours	
Parking	From Balerno follow signs to Marchbank, and car park is on the left, near where the road ends	
Route terrain	Reservoir tracks and rough mountain upland, mainly on grass and heather	
Ordnance Survey maps	Landranger 66 (Edinburgh), Explorer 344 (Pentland Hills)	

GPS waypoints

- ✔ NT 166 639
- Ⓐ NT 165 629
- Ⓑ NT 174 604
- Ⓒ NT 191 611
- Ⓓ NT 195 615
- Ⓔ NT 189 619

A long, lovely and gradual climb from Threipmuir Reservoir across open grassland leads to the main, central ridge of the Pentlands and then follows a splendid but moderately strenuous switchback over three peaks: West Kip, East Kip and finally Scald Law (1,898 feet/579m), the highest point in the Pentland range. As might be expected, the views from the ridge path – to the left across the Pentlands to the Firth of Forth and to the right across the lowlands to the Lammermuir Hills – are magnificent. The descent from Scald Law is followed by an attractive walk through the narrow and steep-sided valley of Green Cleugh to return to the start. This is a most enjoyable and exhilarating walk with plenty of steep climbing and superb views, but definitely one to be avoided in bad weather, especially mist, unless you are experienced in such conditions and able to navigate by using a compass.

West Kip

🥾 Turn left out of the car park along a track and, after a few yards where the track bears left, turn sharp right along a path through trees. On reaching a tarmac drive opposite a notice for Red Moss Nature Reserve, turn left along it to cross Redford Bridge over Threipmuir Reservoir.

Reaching the top of West Kip

Continue along the lovely, uphill beech drive ahead and at a T-junction of tracks **Ⓐ**, turn right at a public footpath sign for Nine Mile Burn and Carlops. After going through a gate, turn left along a drive to a stile, climb it and continue along a track, by a wall and wire fence bordering woodland on the left, to climb another one.

Now follow a track gently uphill, keeping parallel to a wall on the left, onto the open, rolling, heathery expanses of the Pentlands, with grand views of the main Pentland ridge. The track leads up to a gate and footpath sign. Go through, continue to cross a burn and shortly head up more steeply, bending left towards the first of the three summits, West Kip.

On reaching a stile in a wire fence on the right, bear left onto a path **Ⓑ** that heads steeply and a little dauntingly up the smooth, grassy slopes of West Kip. At the top is the reward of a magnificent view that takes in the Pentland ridge, Firth of Forth, the Lothian lowlands and the Lammermuir and Moorfoot Hills. From here the path descends and then ascends – rather less steeply – to the summit of East Kip. Then follows a steep descent to a fork. Here take the left-hand path to climb steeply again to the trig pillar on the summit of Scald Law **Ⓒ**, the highest point in the Pentlands, and an even more magnificent viewpoint.

Continue past the trig pillar and head steeply down into the next dip below the slopes of Carnethy Hill. Where paths cross **Ⓓ**, climb a stile and turn left to head steeply downhill, by a wire fence on the left, to a ladder-stile. Climb it,

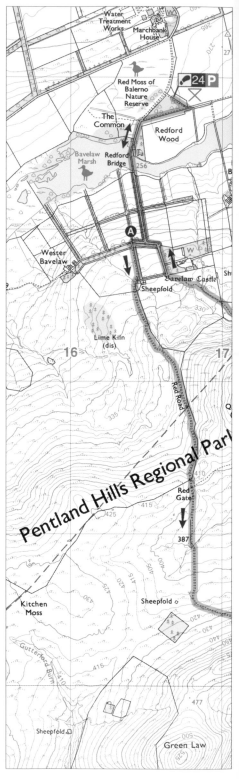

continue along the path that curves right to another stile, climb that and keep ahead steeply downhill. Nearing the bottom, the path swings left down to a stile. Cross it, by a public footpath sign for the Old Kirk Road to Penicuik, keep ahead and turn left at a fence corner **Ⓔ** along a path by a burn on the right. There is a path on each side of the burn – take your pick as either will involve at least one fording.

Continue through the narrow, peaceful, steep-sided valley of Green Cleugh, climbing gently to reach a ladder-stile. Turn left over it to press on along the right-hand side of the valley – the sides are less steep now – climb another ladder-stile and continue towards the trees ahead. The path then turns left to cross a short stretch of marshy ground and winds past two waymarked posts to a ladder-stile on the edge of the trees, by a public foot-path sign for Penicuik, Colinton and Flotterstone.

Climb the stile and continue along a beech drive, following it first to the left and shortly around to the right. Here you rejoin the outward route **Ⓐ** to retrace your steps to the start. ●

Threipmuir Reservoir from Redford Bridge

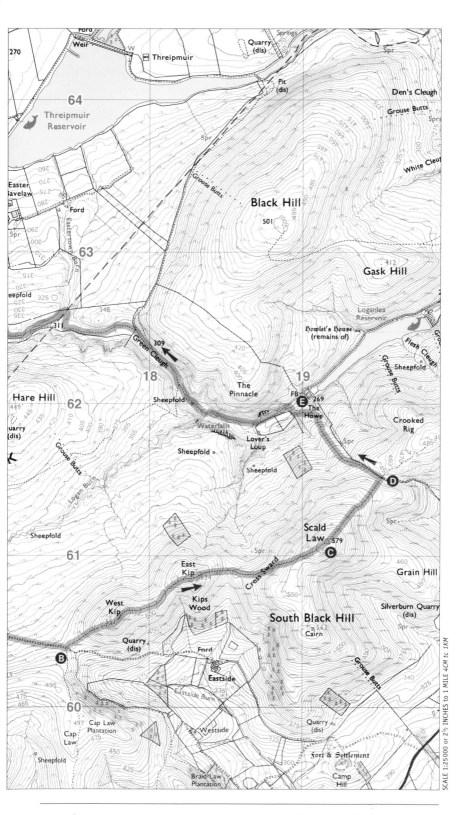

Aberlady Nature Reserve and Gullane Bay

		GPS waypoints
Start	Aberlady Nature Reserve	
Distance	8 miles (13km)	◢ NT 471 805
Height gain	555 feet (170m)	Ⓐ NT 466 817
Approximate time	4 hours	Ⓑ NT 467 831
Parking	At start	Ⓒ NT 482 844
Route terrain	Good paths across coastal dune and rocky coastline	Ⓓ NT 484 846
		Ⓔ NT 486 841
		Ⓕ NT 482 838
		Ⓖ NT 463 828
Ordnance Survey maps	Landranger 67 (Duns, Dunbar & Eyemouth), Explorer 351 (Dunbar & North Berwick)	

Aberlady Bay has the distinction of being Britain's first local nature reserve, so designated in 1952. It is also part of a Site of Special Scientific Interest in recognition of its botanical, ornithological and geomorphologic significance. This walk wanders gently through the reserve to the coastal dunes, heading for Gullane Point, before turning east and following the coastline around Gullane Bay. The walking is of the easiest and most enjoyable kind, and a pair of binoculars to help identify the abundant birdlife will be especially useful.

◢ Set off across the wooden walkway spanning a tidal burn; once across a clear path leads on through the nature reserve, passing Mari Loch, and then enters an area of scrub dominated by orange-berried sea buckthorn. Beyond, the path runs on across the rough ground that forms the heart of the reserve, towards the distant golf course.

Aberlady Local Nature Reserve covers an area of 582 hectares (1,439 acres), of which two-thirds falls below the high-tide mark and consists of tidal sand, mud flats and salt marsh. Aberlady Bay is renowned for its birdlife. In the winter months, several species of wader and duck roost or feed in the area, while at dusk, thousands of pink-footed geese

fly in. Breeding species include skylark, reed bunting, eider, shelduck, lapwing, lesser whitethroat and redshank; willow and sedge warblers are common in most years. By the autumn, up to 10,000 waders are often present, with lapwing and golden plover most common, while numerous wigeon feed in the bay.

The path leads on, and eventually reaches a broad cross track Ⓐ. Here turn left, and follow the track out to reach the coast, where undulating sand dunes predominate. Turn right along the coastline, and walk up to Gullane Point. There are a number of diverging paths, but the simple expedient of following the coast will bring you to the Point. Here turn to the east to reach the

SCALE 1:25000 or 2½ INCHES to 1 MILE 4CM to 1KM

sandy bay at Hummell Rocks **B**. On the cliffs ahead are a group of large cement blocks, anti-tank devices built during

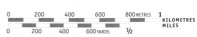

mountain bikes' **C**. Go through this gate and walk by the fence to a track. Bear right on to this and then, opposite a gate, turn left to walk to the summit of Lammer Law with its large cairn and triangulation pillar at 1,729 feet (526m), the highest point of the Lammermuir Hills.

It will have taken about 90 minutes to reach the summit. The view northwards is extensive and it is said that the Cairngorms may be seen in exceptional conditions. Certainly the main landmarks of the Forth coast and estuary are more readily seen.

Turn back to the right of way and turn right to resume walking southwards. The track descends gently to reach a gate **D**. Do not go through the gate but turn to the left to descend over heather to pass a line of butts and reach Harley Grain, a mini-ravine which drops steeply at first to pass through a cordon of thistles and nettles which will not be appreciated by anyone wearing shorts. Once this hazard is passed a path becomes discernible to the left of the burn. This soon reaches the head of a beautiful valley where the walking is on smooth greensward. The path crosses the burn several times and gradually becomes a track, which fords the burn close to a corrugated sheep enclosure and hut. Farther on there are beehives by a similar enclosure.

The track rises above the burn and soon gives a glimpse of the Hopes Reservoir. Look out for herons here. With the reservoir in view the track fords Hopes Water for the last time **E** and runs above the man-made lake; the views are splendid.

After the grass-covered dam the track

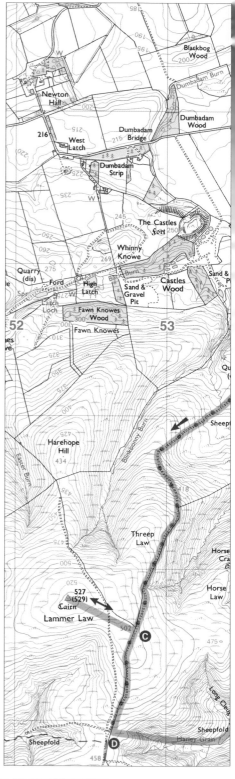

0	200	400	600	800 METRES	1
					KILOMETRES
					MILES
0	200	400	600 YARDS	½	

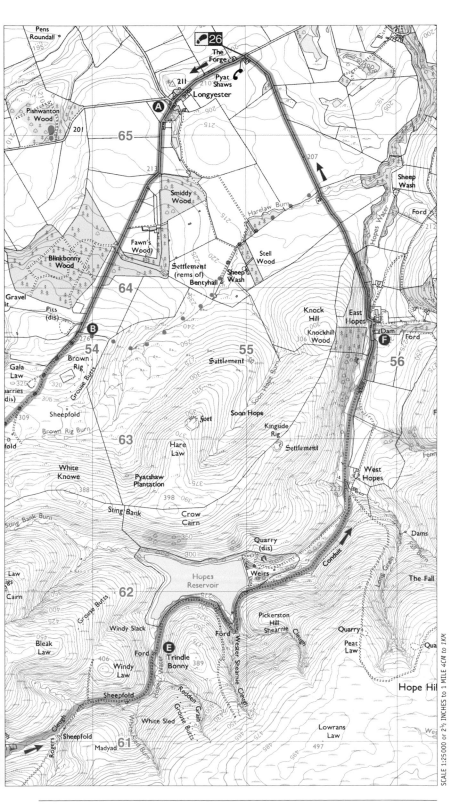

SCALE 1:25000 or 2½ INCHES to 1 MILE 4CM to 1KM

descends to West Hopes giving fine views northwards. The track becomes a surfaced road after a gate at East Hopes, which is a popular place for people to leave their cars **F**. After this the return to Longyester is straightforward walking on about two miles of well-surfaced road.

Hopes Reservoir

Gladhouse Reservoir and the Huntly Cot Hills

		GPS waypoints
Start	Gladhouse Reservoir	✐ NT 309 541
Distance	9 miles (14.5km)	Ⓐ NT 309 530
Height gain	1,130 feet (345m)	Ⓑ NT 316 524
Approximate time	4½ hours	Ⓒ NT 331 527
Parking	Gladhouse Reservoir; there are a number of parking areas to choose from	Ⓓ NT 310 503 Ⓔ NT 297 512
Route terrain	Rough tracks and mountain moorland	
Ordnance Survey maps	Landranger 66 (Edinburgh), Explorer 344 (Pentland Hills)	

The drive around the reservoir to the starting point is not the least of the scenic delights of this route in the Moorfoot Hills, particularly if you are there early in the morning and the sun is shining. The going is over rough ground at times, but once on the hills you are unlikely to meet other walkers and aircraft, birdsong, and the wind in the heather only disturb the silence. Ask locally if you intend to walk the route during the grouse-shooting season (12 August – 10 December).

✐ Continue southwards along the road to pass an Arniston Estates signboard. Before Mauldslie go through the gate ahead when faced with a T-junction Ⓐ. Climb the grassy track with the burn to the right to reach a small clump of trees. It is worth pausing here to take in the view.

Go through the gate at the top and bear slightly left on a faint path heading towards a plantation. The ford shown on the map Ⓑ is midway between the plantation on the left and a small hillock to the right. After the ford the path leads to the top corner of the plantation. From here a clear path climbs gradually up the flank of the hill in an easterly direction heading for a

point above another small plantation. Cross another burn and walk along the edge of bracken, climbing steadily. Having left the plantation behind, a fence comes into view ahead. Climb with this to the left to reach a gate where two fences meet Ⓒ.

Having gone through the gate, turn right to follow the fence south-westwards. You are walking on the boundary between the Lothians and the Borders. A track runs by the fence for most of the way on Mauldslie Hill and there are magnificent views westwards over the reservoir. The view to the left is of lonely, softly moulded hills with no paths or tracks obvious. A fence comes up from the right. Continue on the path

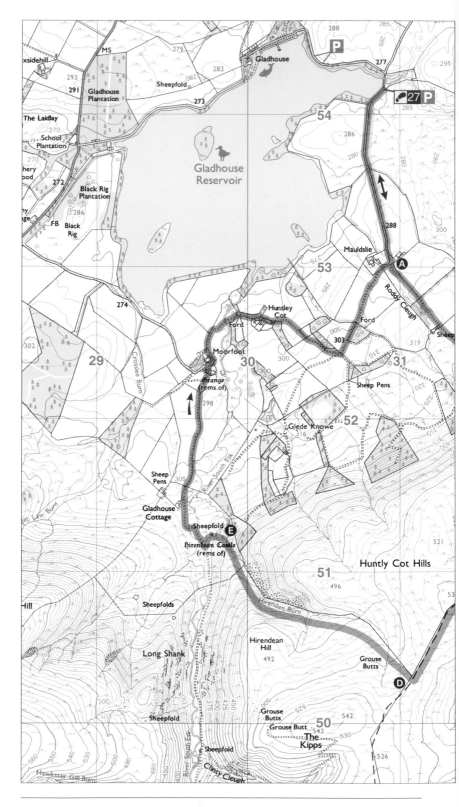

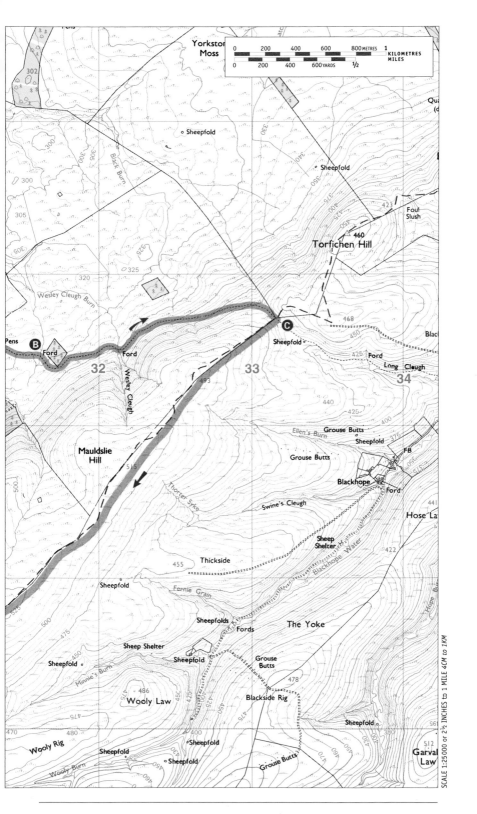

Huntly Cot

When a second fence joins on the right, pass through (or over) the gate **D**, and walk down over rough heather with the fence to the right. Pass to the right of shooting butts taking care over moist, tussocky ground. A burn steadily grows in strength to the right and provides pools where cool waters will soothe aching feet. A path becomes discernible by the burn, though this probably owes more to sheep than to man.

Take care when the descent becomes steep and rocky with the stream passing to the other side of the fence and dropping down cascades. The path is now clear and the ruins of Hirendean Castle soon come into view. Pass both the castle **E** and the circular brick-built sheep fold, and then descend to the track. Turn right on to this track and cross the burn.

The track leads to Moorfoot farmyard. Bear right here to follow the signpost to Huntly Cottage. The remainder of the route is on well-signed farm tracks leading back to Mauldslie and the road, which takes you back to the start.   ●

across the Huntly Cot Hills where the imperceptible summit is at 1,742 feet (531m).

The glow of sunset kisses the south Esk Valley

Dunbar Common and the Herring Road

Dunbar Common and the Herring Road

		GPS waypoints
Start	Pressmennan Wood	🔖 NT 621 726
Distance	11¼ miles (18km)	Ⓐ NT 614 713
Height gain	1,625 feet (495m)	Ⓑ NT 632 661
Approximate time	6 hours	Ⓒ NT 637 656
Parking	Pressmennan Wood car park. From Stenton, take the lane signposted to Deuchrie and, just after Rucklaw West Mains Farm, turn left onto a track at a 'Forest Trail Car Park' sign	Ⓓ NT 648 689
Route terrain	Rough moorland	
Ordnance Survey maps	Landranger 67 (Duns, Dunbar & Eyemouth), Explorers 345 (Lammermuir Hills) and 351 (Dunbar & North Berwick)	

The Lammermuir Hills are a range of rolling, open, heathery moorland, rising to over 1,700 feet (518m) and from their northern slopes there are superb and extensive views over the fertile lowlands of Lothian and along the North Sea coast. This walk over the Lammermuirs is a lengthy but not strenuous walk as all the ascents and descents are long and gradual, and most of the route is along clear and well-surfaced tracks, with just two difficult sections where the track degenerates into a rough, faint and uneven path. It is exhilarating to walk across these wide and empty expanses, and the views are magnificent, but this is a walk best reserved for a fine and clear day; in bad weather and misty conditions route-finding could be difficult in places.

🔖 Start by walking back along the track to the lane, turn left and follow it for one mile around several sharp bends and over a wooden footbridge. At a row of cottages on the left, turn left Ⓐ along an uphill tarmac drive to Stoneypath Farm and by the farm turn right through a metal gate, at a public footpath sign to Johnscleugh, to continue along a steadily ascending track. Ahead are grand views over the smooth, heathery slopes of the

Lammermuirs, a foretaste of pleasures to come.

Follow the track steadily uphill across Clints Dod. Cross a track just to the right of a house, continue by a wire fence on the left, go through a gate and proceed over the open moorland. After reaching the summit – virtually imperceptible – the track descends gently to a gate. Go through and continue steadily downhill into the Whiteadder Valley. Go through a gate,

A view of the Lammermuir Hills

keep ahead to pass between the buildings of Johnscleugh Farm and continue along a downhill track. Where the track bends sharply to the right, keep ahead steeply downhill. Ford Whiteadder Water – might be difficult after a rainy spell – and continue along an uphill path to a lane **B**.

Turn left for ½ mile above the winding Whiteadder Water and, just after first a left- and then a right-hand bend, you reach a bridge beyond which is a cattle-grid **C**. Here turn left along a broad track; this is the Herring Road, an ancient highway across the hills that linked the fishing port of Dunbar with its markets inland. Recross the Whiteadder, this time by a footbridge, go through a gate and press on along the broad, winding, uphill track. The track later straightens out and, where it bends right, continue by a wire fence on the left across the moorland. Go through a gate, keep ahead and, after the fence turns left, continue across rough grass to join and walk along a clear, well-constructed track again.

A few yards after going through a gate to the right of a small group of conifers, the track bears right. Keep straight ahead here across rough grass and heather to climb a stile by a public footpath sign. Continue in the same direction, following a broad swathe of heather and rough grass through a conifer plantation to reach a stony track by two public footpath signs. Cross the track, continue along a reasonably discernible path through the conifers and, soon after descending to cross a small burn, head up a steep embankment to a public footpath sign in front of a metal gate and by a fence corner and broken wall. Go through the gate and continue uphill, by a wire fence on the left, to the fence corner.

Turn left **D**, here leaving the Herring Road, to walk across open moorland along a grassy path by a fence, still bordering a plantation on the left. At the corner of the plantation, go through a gate and keep ahead, still by a fence on the left, across the wide-open expanses of Dunbar Common. Pass through a metal gate, continue and after the fence on the left ends keep straight ahead across moorland. At this point the path is unclear in places, and there is some rough and difficult walking, but keep in a straight line all the while until a discernible path reappears, and later still a clear, grassy track emerges. All the way there are magnificent views across the lowlands to the coast, with both North Berwick Law and Traprain Law standing out prominently.

Eventually the grassy track heads downhill, curving left and descending more steeply to go through a fence gap to the right of a circular sheepfold. Continue downhill, pass to the left of a house to reach a gate, go through and head uphill to Deuchrie Farm. Go through a metal gate, pass between the house and farm buildings and continue along a tarmac drive to reach a lane at a bend. Retrace your steps to the start. ●

SCALE 1:33333 or 1⅞ INCHES to 1 MILE 3CM to 1KM

0   200   400   600   800 METRES 1
                                         KILOMETRES
                                         MILES
0   200   400   600 YARDS ½

Further Information

 Walkers and the Law

Walkers in Scotland have long enjoyed a moral and de facto right of access. Nothing much has changed except that this is now enshrined in *The Land Reform (Scotland) Act 2003*. The Act tells you where you have right of access and *The Scottish Outdoor Access Code* sets out your responsibilities when exercising your rights. These rights came into effect on 9 February 2005.

Walkers following the routes in this book should not have any problems but it is as well to know something about the law as it affects access, particularly as the legislation in Scotland is significantly different from elsewhere in Britain. Mostly, though, it's just common sense. Be considerate to other land users, look after the places you visit and take responsibility for your own safety.

The Scottish Outdoor Access Code

1. Take responsibility for your own actions.
2. Respect people's privacy and peace of mind. When close to a house or garden, keep a sensible distance from the house, use a path or track if there is one, and take extra care at night.
3. Help land managers and others to work safely and effectively. Do not hinder land management operations and follow advice from land managers. Respect requests for reasonable limitations on when and where you can go.
4. Care for your environment. Do not disturb wildlife, leave the environment as you find it and follow a path or track if there is one.
5. Keep your dog under proper control. Do not take it through fields of calves and lambs, and dispose of dog dirt.
6. Take extra care if you are organising an event or running a business and ask the landowner's advice.

Some fairly comprehensive guidance is available at:
www.outdooraccess-scotland.com

The following covers some of the most common situations affecting walkers.

Car Parking

Motorised vehicles are not included in the access rights, but most people will use a vehicle to reach the start of a walk. It's important to park sensibly and avoid causing an obstruction. Use a car park if one is nearby. If not, make sure you do not block the entrance to a field or building, make it difficult for other road users or damage the verge.

Dogs

Dog walkers are covered by the legislation provided they keep their dogs under control at all times. Avoid fields with sheep during the lambing season (spring). During the bird-breeding season (April – July) keep your dog on a lead while near breeding habitats. Where crossing fields containing animals keep your dog on a short lead.

Farm Steadings

There is no legal right of access to farm steadings. In practice though many tracks and paths do go through farm steadings and you should consider the following advice:

If a right of way or core path goes through the steading then you can follow that.

If an alternative route has been signposted round the steading then it should be used. If the route through the steading has been taken on a customary basis you may be able to continue to do so.

You may go through the steading if the farmer gives you permission. Otherwise you will have to exercise your legal right to go around the farm steading and buildings.

Whatever route you use through, or round, a farm steading exercise care, avoid machinery and livestock and respect the privacy of people living on the farm.

Fields

Keep to paths where possible or walk

Glossary of Gaelic Names

Many of the place names in Scotland are Gaelic in origin, and this list gives some of the more common elements, which will allow readers to understand otherwise meaningless words and appreciate the relationship between place names and landscape features. Place names often have variant spellings, and the more common of these are given here.

aber	mouth of loch, river	eilidh	hind
abhainn	river	eòin, eun	bird
allt	stream	fionn	white
auch, ach	field	fraoch	heather
bal, bail, baile	town, homestead	gabhar, ghabhar,	
bàn	white, fair, pale	gobhar	goat
bealach	hill pass	garbh	rough
beg, beag	small	geal	white
ben, beinn	hill	ghlas, glas	grey
bhuidhe	yellow	gleann, glen	narrow, valley
blar	plain	gorm	blue, green
brae, braigh	upper slope, steepening	inbhir, inver	confluence
		inch, inis, innis	island, meadow by river
breac	speckled		
cairn	pile of stones, often marking a summit	lag, laggan	hollow
		làrach	old site
cam	crooked	làirig	pass
càrn	cairn, cairn-shaped hill	leac	slab
		liath	grey
caol, kyle	strait	loch	lake
ceann, ken, kin	head	lochan	small loch
cil, kil	church, cell	màm	pass, rise
clach	stone	maol	bald-shaped top
clachan	small village	monadh	upland, moor
cnoc	hill, knoll, knock	mór, mor(e)	big
coille, killie	wood	odhar, odhair	dun-coloured
corrie, coire,		rhu, rubha	point
choire	mountain hollow	ruadh	red, brown
craig, creag	cliff, crag	sgòr, sgòrr,	
crannog,		sgùrr	pointed
crannag	man-made island	sron	nose
dàl, dail	field, flat	stob	pointed
damh	stag	strath	valley (broader than glen)
dearg	red		
druim, drum	long ridge	tarsuinn	traverse, across
dubh, dhu	black, dark	tom	hillock (rounded)
dùn	hill fort	tòrr	hillock (more rugged)
cas	waterfall	tulloch, tulach	knoll
eilean	island	uisge	water, river

around the margins of a field under crops. Bear in mind that grass is also grown as a crop. Where fields have been sprayed there are occasions when the landowner has a responsibility to keep people out for health and safety reasons for anything from a few hours to three or four days. Obey any signs

or advice from the landowner and work out an alternative route, perhaps through an adjacent field.

Golf Courses

You have a right of access to cross golf courses, but must avoid damage to the

Further Information

playing surface and never step onto the greens. Cross as quickly as possible but consider the rights of the players at the same time. Wait for players to play their shot before crossing the fairway; if you're close to someone about to play, stop and stand still. Keep to any paths that exist and keep dogs on a short lead.

Deer Stalking

During the hunting season walkers should check to ensure that the walks they are planning avoid deer stalking operations.

Culling is an essential part of the management of a sustainable deer population and to avoid overgrazing and damage to fragile habitats.

The red stag stalking season is from 1 July to 20 October, hinds are culled from 21 October to 15 February. September and October tend to be the busiest months. The roe buck stalking season is from 1 April to 20 October, with June to August seeing the peak of activity. The doe-stalking season is from 21 October to 31 March.

During the busy periods of the season stalking can take place six days of the week but never on a Sunday.

The easiest way to find out if the walk you are planning is affected is to refer to the Hillphones website www.snh.org.uk/hillphones. Here you can find a map of the phones and the relevant numbers. Calls are charged at normal rates and you will hear a recorded message that is changed each morning.

Grouse Shooting

The season runs from 12 August to 10 December. During this period please follow any advice regarding alternative routes on grouse moors to minimise disturbance to the shoot. Avoid crossing land where a shoot is in progress until it is absolutely safe to do so.

Safety on the Hills

The hills, mountains and moorlands of Britain, though of modest height compared

with those in many other countries, need to be treated with respect. Friendly and inviting in good weather, they can quickly be transformed into wet, misty, windswept and potentially dangerous areas of wilderness in bad weather. Even on an outwardly fine and settled summer day, conditions can rapidly deteriorate at high altitudes and, in winter, even more so.

Therefore it is advisable to always take both warm and waterproof clothing, sufficient nourishing food, a hot drink, first-aid kit, torch and whistle. Wear suitable footwear, such as strong walking boots or shoes that give a good grip over rocky terrain and on slippery slopes. Try to obtain a local weather forecast and bear it in mind before you start. Do not be afraid to abandon your proposed route and return to your starting point in the event of a sudden and unexpected deterioration in the weather. Do not go alone and allow enough time to finish the walk well before nightfall.

Most of the walks described in this book do not venture into remote wilderness areas and will be safe to do, given due care and respect, at any time of year in all but the most unreasonable weather. Indeed, a crisp, fine winter day often provides perfect walking conditions, with firm ground underfoot and a clarity that is not possible to achieve in the other seasons of the year. A few walks, however, are suitable only for reasonably fit and experienced hill walkers able to use a compass and should definitely not be tackled by anyone else during the winter months or in bad weather, especially high winds and mist. These are indicated in the general description that precedes each of the walks.

Useful Organisations

Association for the Protection of Rural Scotland
Gladstone's Land, 3rd Floor,
483 Lawnmarket, Edinburgh EH1 2NT
Tel. 0131 225 7012
www.ruralscotland.org.uk

Forestry Commission Scotland
Silvan House,
231 Corstorphine Road, Edinburgh EH12 7AT
Tel. 0131 334 0303
www.forestry.gov.uk/scotland

Historic Scotland
Longmore House, Salisbury Place,
Edinburgh EH9 1SH
Tel. 0131 668 8600
www.historic-scotland.gov.uk

National Trust for Scotland
Wemyss House, 28 Charlotte Square,
Edinburgh EH2 4ET
Tel. 0844 493 2100
www.nts.org.uk

Ordnance Survey
Romsey Road, Maybush,
Southampton SO16 4GU
Tel. 08456 05 05 05
www.ordnancesurvey.co.uk

Ramblers' Association (Scotland)
Kingfisher House, Auld Mart Business Park,
Milnathort, Kinross KY13 9DA
Tel. 01577 861222
www.ramblers.org.uk/scotland

Royal Society for the Protection of Birds
(Scotland)
Dunedin House, 25 Ravelston Terrace
Edinburgh EH4 3TP
Tel. 0131 311 6500
www.rspb.org.uk/scotland

Scottish Natural Heritage
Great Glen House, Leachkin Road,
Inverness IV3 8NW
Tel. 01463 725000
www.snh.gov.uk

Scottish Rights of Way & Access Society
24 Annandale Street, Edinburgh EH7 4AN
Tel. 0131 558 1222
www.scotways.com

Scottish Rural Property and
Business Association
Stuart House, Eskmills Business Park
Musselburgh EH21 7PB
Tel. 0131 653 5400
www.slf.org.uk

Scottish Wildlife Trust
Cramond House, 3
KirkCramond, Edinburgh EH4 6HZ
Tel. 0131 312 7765
www.swt.org.uk

Scottish Youth Hostels Assocation
7 Glebe Crescent, Stirling FK8 2JA
Tel. 01786 891400
www.syha.org.uk

Tourist Information Scotland
VisitScotland
Level 3, Ocean Point 1,
94 Ocean Drive, Edinburgh
EH6 6JH
Tel. 0131 472 2222
www.visitscotland.com

Local tourist information offices
Dunbar: 01368 863 353
North Berwick: 01620 892 197

 ## Ordnance Survey maps of Edinburgh, Pentlands and Lothians

This area is covered by Ordnance Survey
1:50 000 scale (1 ¼ inches to 1 mile or 2cm
to 1km) Landranger map sheets 65, 66, and
67. These all-purpose maps are packed with
information to help you explore the area.
Viewpoints, picnic sites, places of interest,
caravan and camping sites are shown, as
well as public rights of way information
such as footpaths and bridleways.

To examine the Edinburgh, Pentlands
and Lothians in more detail, and especially
if you are planning walks, Ordnance Survey
Explorer maps 344, 345, 349, 350 and 351
at 1:25 000 (2 ½ inches to 1 mile or 4cm to
1km) scale are ideal.

To get to Edinburgh, Pentlands and
Lothians use the Ordnance Survey Travel
Map-Route Great Britain at 1:625 000 (1
inch to 10 miles or 4cm to 35km) scale or
Ordnance Survey Travel Map - Road 3
(Southern Scotland and Northumberland) at
1:250 000 (1 inch to 4 miles or 1 cm to
2.5km) scale.

Ordnance Survey maps and guides are
available from most booksellers, stationers
and newsagents.

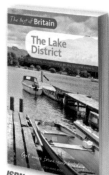